ADVANCES IN IMAGE SEGMENTATION

Edited by **Pei-Gee Peter Ho**

Advances in Image Segmentation
http://dx.doi.org/10.5772/3425
Edited by Pei-Gee Peter Ho

Contributors

Saïd Mahmoudi, Mohammed Benjelloun, Mohamed Amine Larhmam, Vallejos, Silvia Ojeda, Roberto Rodriguez, Pradipta Kumar Nanda, Luciano Lulio

Published by InTech

Janeza Trdine 9, 51000 Rijeka, Croatia

Publishing Process Manager Martina Blecic
Technical Editor InTech DTP team
Cover InTech Design team

Additional hard copies can be obtained from orders@intechopen.com

Advances in Image Segmentation, Edited by Pei-Gee Peter Ho
p. cm.
ISBN 978-953-51-0817-7

For EU product safety concerns:
IN TECH d.o.o., Prolaz Marije Krucifikse Kozulić 3, 51000 Rijeka, Croatia,
info@intechopen.com or visit our website at intechopen.com.

Meet the editor

Dr. Pei-Gee Peter Ho received his BSEE from National Cheng Kung University, Taiwan in 1976 and MSEE from University of Massachusetts at Dartmouth in 1981. During the last 20 plus years he has worked in various computer engineering companies. He received his Ph.D. degree in EE from UMass Dartmouth in January 2008. He is now working in the DSP algorithm group of Naval Undersea Warfare Center at Newport, Rhode Island and has published four books and a few journal papers in the area of image processing and acoustic digital communications.

Contents

Preface

Generally speaking, image processing applications for computer vision consist of enhancement, reconstruction, segmentation, recognition and communications. In the last few years, image segmentation played an important role in image analysis.

The field of digital image segmentation is continually evolving. Most recently, the advanced segmentation methods such as Template Matching, Spatial and Temporal ARMA Processes, Mean Shift Iterative Algorithm, Constrained Compound Markov Random Field (CCMRF) model and Statistical Pattern Recognition (SPR) methods form the core of a modernization effort that resulted in the current text. In the medical world, it is interested to detect and extract vertebra locations from X-ray images. The generalized Hough Transform to detect vertebra positions and orientations is proposed. The spatial autoregressive moving average (ARMA) processes have been extensively used in several applications in image and signal processing. In particular, these models have been used for image segmentation. The Mean shift (MSH) method is a robust technique which has been applied in many computer vision tasks. The MSH procedure moves to a kernel-weighted average of the observations within a smoothing window. This computation is repeated until convergence is obtained at a local density mode. The density modes can be located without explicitly estimating. The Constrained Markov Random Field (MRF) model has the unifying property of modeling scene as well as texture images. The scheme is specifically meant to preserve weak edges besides the well defined strong edges. By Statistical Pattern Recognition approach, the cognitive and statistical classifiers were implemented in order to verify the estimated and chosen regions on unstructured environments images.

Following our previous popular artificial intelligent book "Image Segmentation", ISBN 978-953-307-228-9, published on April 19, 2011, this new edition of "Advanced Image Segmentation" is but a reflection of the significant progress that has been made in the field of image segmentation in just the past few years. The book presented chapters that highlight frontier works in image information processing. I am pleased to have leaders in the field to prepare and contribute their most current research and development work. Although no attempt is made to cover every topic, these entire five special chapters shall give readers a deep insight. All topics listed are equal important and significant.

Pei-Gee Peter Ho
DSP Algorithm and Software Design Group,
Naval Undersea Warfare Center
Newport, Rhode Island, USA

Chapter 1

Template Matching Approaches Applied to Vertebra Detection

Mohammed Benjelloun, Saïd Mahmoudi and
Mohamed Amine Larhmam

Additional information is available at the end of the chapter

http://dx.doi.org/10.5772/50476

1. Introduction

In the medical world, the problems of back and spine are usually inseparable. They can take various forms ranging from the low back pain to scoliosis and osteoporosis. Medical Imaging provides very useful information about the patient's condition, and the adopted treatment depends on the symptoms described and the interpretation of this information. This information is generally analyzed visually and subjectively by a human expert. In this difficult task, medical images processing presents an effective aid able to help medical staff. This is nowhere clearer than in diagnostics and therapy in the medical world.

We are particularly interested to detect and extract vertebra locations from X-ray images. Some works related to this field can be found in the literature. Actually, these contributions are mainly interested in only 2 medical imagery modalities: Computed Tomography (CT) and Magnetic Resonance (MR). A few works are dedicated to the conventional X-Ray radiography. However, this modality is the cheapest and fastest one to obtain spine images. In addition, from the point of view of the patient, this procedure has the advantage to be more safe and non-invasive. For these reasons, this review is widely used and remains essential treatments and/or urgent diagnosis. Despite these valuable benefits, the interpretation of images of this type remains a difficult task now. Their nature is the main cause. Indeed, in practice, these images are characterized by a low contrast and it is not uncommon that some parts of the image are partially hidden by other organs of the human body. As a result, the vertebra edge is not always obvious to see or detect.

In the context of cervical spinal column analysis, the vertebra edges detection task is very useful for further processing, like angular measures (between two consecutive vertebrae or in the same vertebra in several images), vertebral mobility analysis and motion estimation. However, automatically detecting vertebral bodies in X-Ray images is a very complex task, especially because of the noise and the low contrast resulting in that kind of medical imagery modality. The goal of this work is to provide some computer vision tools that enable to measure vertebra movement and to determine the mobility of each vertebra compared to others in the same image.

The main idea of the proposed work in this chapter is to locate vertebra positions in radiographs. This operation is an essential preliminary pre-processing step used to achieve full automatic vertebra segmentation. The goal of the segmentation process is to exploit only the useful information for image interpretation. The reader is lead to discover [1] for an overview of the current segmentation methods applied to medical imagery. The vertebra segmentation has already been treated in various ways. The level set method is a numerical technique used for the evolution of curves and surfaces in a discrete domain [2]. The advantage is that the edge has not to be parameterized and the topology changes are automatically taken into account. Some works related to the vertebrae are presented in [3]. The active contour algorithm deforms and moves a contour submitted to internal and external energies [4]. A special case, the Discrete Dynamic Contour Model [5] has been applied to the vertebra segmentation in [6]. A survey on deformable models is done in [7]. Other methods exist and without being exhaustive, let's just mention the parametric methods [15], or the use boundary based segmentation [16] and also Watershed based segmentation approaches [17].

The difficulties resulting from the use of X-ray images force the segmentation methods to be as robust as possible. In this chapter, we propose, in the first part, some methods that we have already used for extracting vertebrae and the results obtained. The second part will focus on a new method, using the Hough transform to detect vertebrae locations. Indeed, the proposed method is based on the application of the Generalized Hough Transform in order to detect vertebra positions and orientations. For this task, we propose first, to use a detection method based on the Generalized Hough Transform and in addition, we propose a cost function in order to eliminate the false positives shapes detected. This function is based on vertebra positions and orientations on the image.

This chapter is organized as follow: In section 02 we present some of our previous works composed of two category of method. The firsts are based on a preliminary region selection process followed by a second segmentation step. We have proposed three segmentation approach based on corner detection, polar signature and vertebral faces detection. The second category of methods proposed in this chapter is based on the active shape model theory. In section 03 we describe a new automatic vertebrae detection approach based on the Generalized Hough transform. In section 04 we conclude this chapter.

2. Previous work

In this part, we provide an overview of the segmentation approach methods that we have already applied to vertebrae detection and segmentation. We proposed two kinds of segmentation approaches. The first one were based a regions selection process allowing the detection of vertebra orientations and inter-vertebral angles and the second based of the active shape model theory. These methods present semi-automatic computer based techniques.

2.1. Region selection

In this section, we propose a first pre-processing step which allows the creation of a polygonal region for each vertebra. This pre-treatment is achieved by a template matching approach based on a mathematical representation of the inter-vertebral area. Indeed, each region represents a specific geometrical model based on the geometry and the orientation of the vertebra. We suggest a supervised process where the user has to click once at the center of each vertebra to be analyzed. These clicks represent the starting points $P(x_i, y_i)$ for the construction of vertebra regions [11]. After this, we compute the distance between every two contiguous points ($D_{i,i+1}$) and the line L1, which connects these contiguous points, by a first order polynomial, equation (1).

$$L_1 = f\left[a, b; P(x_i, y_i), P(x_{i+1}, y_{i+1})\right] \tag{1}$$

The function L1 will be used as reference for a template displacement, Figure 1, by the function T(x,y) defined in equation (2). This template function represents an inter vertebral model, which is calculated according to the shapes of the areas between vertebrae.

$$T(x, y) = \left(1 - e^{-r x_i^2}\right) with r = \frac{k}{D_{i,i+1}} \tag{2}$$

With k = 0.1 an empirical value and xi the coordinate of the point (x, y) in the new reference plane in each vertebra center. We use the L1 function and the inter-vertebral distances, to compute the inter-vertebral angles (αiv) and to determine a division line for each inter-vertebral area. The goal of this proposed template matching process is to find the positions on the image which are best correlated with the template function. So, for each vertebra, the template function $T(x, y)$ is first placed on the geometrical inter-vertebral central point $P(x_{ic}, y_{ic})$, which represents the average position between each two contiguous click points: $P(x_i, y_i)$ and$P(x_{i+1}, y_{i+1})$. The new reference plane -on each vertebra- is created with the point $P(x_{ic}, y_{ic})$ as center. The X axis of this plane is the line L1. The Y axis is therefore easily created by tracing the line passing through $P(x_{ic}, y_{ic})$and orthogonal to L1. We notice that the orientation angle of this second axis present the initial value of the orientation angle αiv.

To determine the points representing border areas, we displace the template function $T(x, y)$ equation (2), between every two reference points $P(x_i, y_i)$and $P(x_{i+1}, y_{i+1})$, along the line L1. For more details on this approach, the reader can consult this [8]. The results obtained by the process of vertebral regions selection are shown in Fig 2.

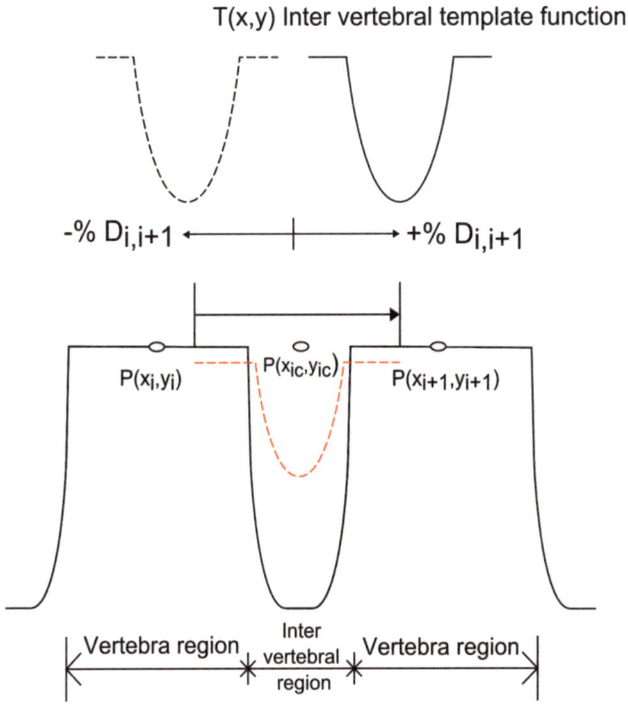

Figure 1. The template function T displacement.

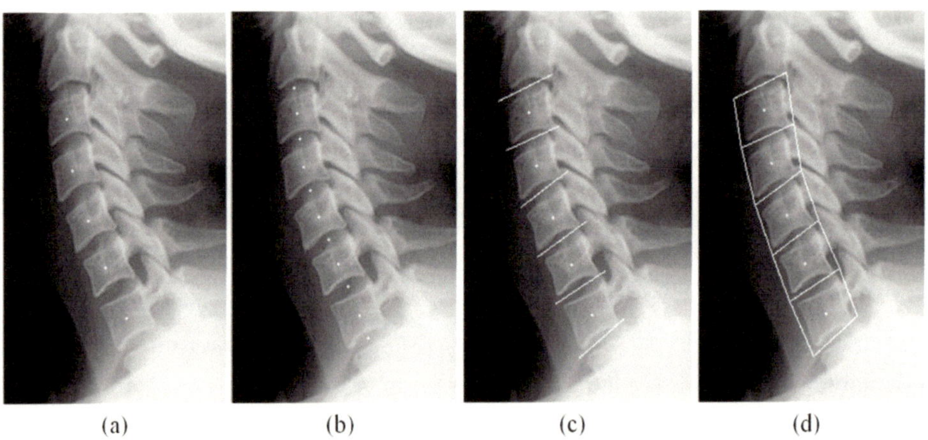

Figure 2. Results obtained by the process of vertebral regions selection. (a) Original image reference with the click points, (b) inter-vertebral points given by the template matching process, (c) boundary lines between vertebrae, (d) vertebrae regions.

2.1.1. Harris corner detector

After the creation of a polygonal area for each vertebra, we can apply locally a few approaches to segmentation as shown in the following examples.

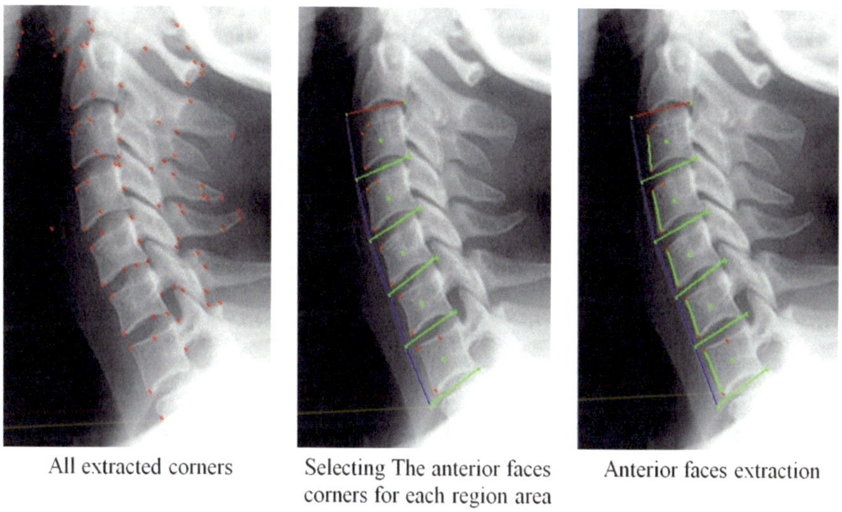

Figure 3. The different steps of the detection process using the region selection method combined to the Harris corner detector.

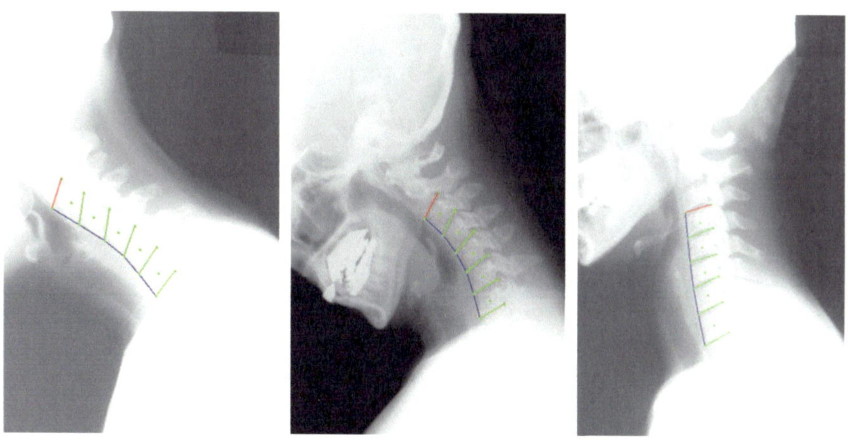

Figure 4. Results obtained by using the region selection method combined to the Harris corner detector.

Figure 3 and figure 4 show the results obtained by using the region selection method combined to the Harris corner detector [8] applied to X-ray image of the cervical spinal column. We notice that the process of region selection, Figure 3, gives very good results and permit to isolate each vertebra separately in a polygonal area. On the other hand, the extraction of the anterior face of the vertebra using the interest point detection process is given with high precision.

2.1.2. Polar signature

A second segmentation approach that we proposed to apply after the region selection process is based on a polar signature [8] representation associated to the polygonal region for each vertebra described on section 2.1. We choose to use this approach in order to explore all region points likely to be corresponding to vertebra contours.

For each vertebra we use as center of the polar coordinate system the click point initially used for the region selection step. For the beginning direction, we chose the average direction between the frontal line direction and the posterior line. We rotate the radial vector 360° around the central points with a step parameter expressed in degrees. In order to determine vertebra contours, we select the maximum value of the image gradient, Figure 5, for each degree inside the research zone.

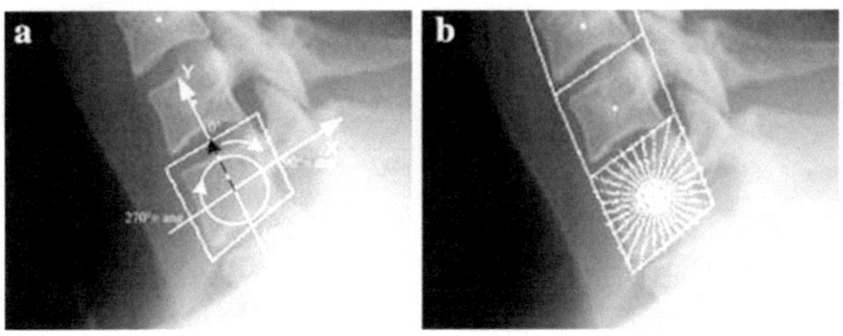

Polar signature system | Polar signature direction

Figure 5. Polar signature applied to vertebra region.

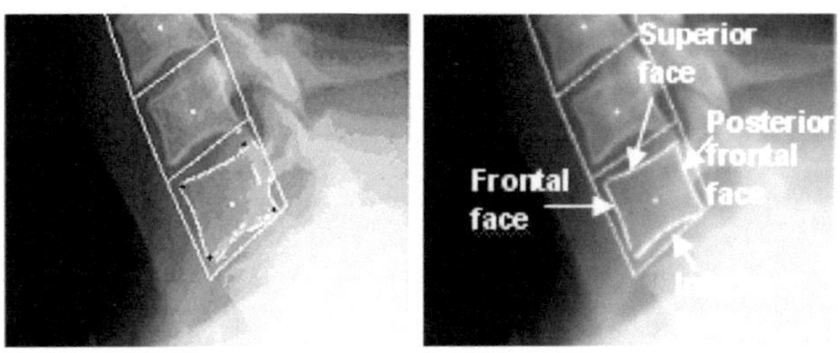

Contour and corners points | Polynomial fitting for each vertebra face

Figure 6. Polynomial fitting applied after a polar signature.

In order to get a closed contour, we apply an edge closing method to the contours obtained, a polynomial fitting to each face for each vertebra. Indeed, for a better approximation of vertebra contours, we use a second degree polynomial fitting [9, 10]. We achieve this 2D polynomial fitting by the least square method, Figure 6.

2.1.3. Vertebral Faces Detection

In this method, we proceed by detecting the four faces belonging to vertebrae contours. We propose an individual characterization of each vertebra by a set of four faces, (anterior, posterior, inferior and superior faces). We start with a process of region selection. The resulting regions obtained are used to create a global polygonal area for each vertebra. Another stage considered as a second pre-treatment step is the computation of the image gradient magnitude on vertebrae regions. This process allows a first approximation of the areas belonging to vertebrae contours, figure 7. To extract faces vertebrae contours, we propose a template matching process based on a mathematical representation of vertebrae by a template function. This function is defined according to the radial intensity distribution on each vertebra. For more details see [12].

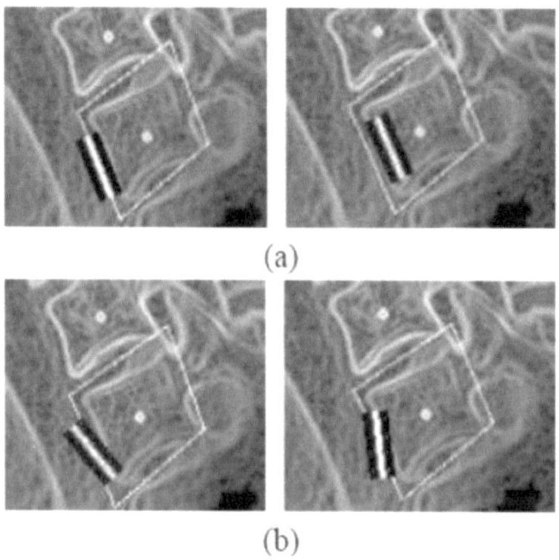

Figure 7. The template matching process for faces detection. (a) translation and, (b) rotation operation applied to the template function.

2.2. Active shape model based segmentation:

In this section, we describe another method that we proposed for cervical vertebra segmentation in digitized X-ray images. This segmentation approach is based on Active Shape Model method [12, 13,14] whose main advantage is that it uses a statistical model. This model is created by training it with sample images on which the boundaries of the object of interest are annotated by an expert. The specialist knowledge is very useful in this context. This model represents the local statistics around each landmark. Our application allows the manipulation of a vertebra model. We proposed an approach which consists on modelling all the shapes of vertebrae by only one vertebra model. The results obtained are very promising. Indeed, the multiple tests which we carried out on a large dataset composed of varied images prove the effectiveness of the suggested approach. The ASM method is composed of 4 steps (figure8):

1. Learning: placing landmarks on the images in order to describe the vertebrae.
2. Model Design: aligning all the marked shapes for the creation of the model.

3. Initialization: the mean shape model is associated with the corners of the searched vertebrae. This step can be manual or semi-automatic.

4. Segmentation: each point of the mean shape evolves so that its contour fits the edge of the vertebrae.

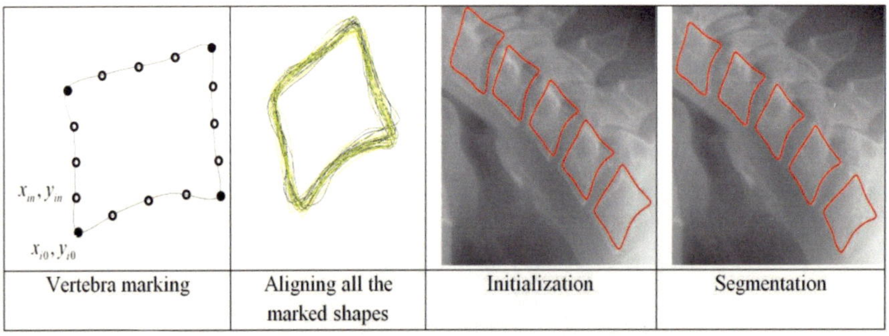

Figure 8. The steps of our framework using ASM.

3. Shape detection using Generalized Hough Transform

In this section, we propose a cervical vertebrae detection method using a modified template matching approach based on the Generalized Hough Transform [18]. The Hough Transform is an interesting technique used in image analysis to extract imperfect instances of a shape in images by a voting procedure. The success of this method relies mainly on the quality of the pattern used. The detection process that we propose starts with the determination of the edges on the radiography. We achieve this task by using the well-known Canny detector, [19]. After this step, the detection algorithm selects among the edges which one look the most similar to the vertebra shape by using the Generalized Hough Transform (GHT) accumulator.

For our experiments, we used 40 X-Ray radiographs coming from the NHANES II database. These images were chosen randomly but they all are focused on the cervical vertebrae C3 to C7. The first pre-processing step consists on a preliminary contour detection step. For this task we used the canny filter detector. After applying the detection process using the GHT method and the cost function proposed, all the vertebrae were detected perfectly. The segmentation results show that vertebra positions and edges are well detected by applying the proposed segmentation approach using the Generalized Hough Transform and followed by applying the proposed cost function.

3.1. Generalized Hough Transform

3.1.1. R-Table construction

The Generalized Hough transform (GHT) is a powerful pattern recognition technique widely used in computer vision. It was initially developed to detect analytic curves (lines, circles, parabolas, etc.) from binary image and extended by D. H. Ballard [18] to extract arbitrary shapes based on a template matching approach. This method is well known by its invariance to scale change, rotation and translation. The detection process of the GHT is presented as two main parts:

The R-Table is a discrete lookup table made to represent the model shape. The construction of this table is computed during a training phase based on the edge information as follow.

Given an arbitrary shape of a target object, figure 11, the first step is to determine a reference point$\vec{c}=(c_x, c_y)$ in the object. The shape is defined in according to the distance and angle from the boundary to the reference point. For each point of the boundary we compute the orientation φ and the relative position $\vec{r}=(r_x, r_y)$ from the reference point. Then, we store the distance r and the direction from the boundary point to the reference point β in the R-Table as a function of the orientationφ. We have in general many occurrences of the same orientation as we move around the boundary. The form of the R-table is shown in Table 1.

Orientation φ	**Positions (r,β)**
0	$\{(r_i, \beta_i) / \varphi_i = 0\}$
$\Delta\varphi$	$\{(r_i, \beta_i) / \varphi_i = \Lambda\varphi\}$
$2\Delta\varphi$	$\{(r_i, \beta_i) / \varphi_i = 2\Delta\varphi\}$
...	...

Table 1. The general R-table form.

3.1.2. The accumulator construction

The accumulator is a three dimensional voting scheme constructed in the following manner. For each edge point $\vec{p}$ in the image, we compute the gradient directionφ_p. Then, we vote for all possible positions $\vec{p}-\vec{r}_i$ of the reference point in the accumalator array, where $\vec{r}_i$ are the positions (r_i, β_i) undexed under $\varphi_i=\varphi_p$in the R-Table. The shape is indicated by finding local maxima in the voting scheme.

3.2. Application to vertebrae segmentation

The proposed approach is based on three main steps:

1. Modeling
2. Detection
3. Post-processing

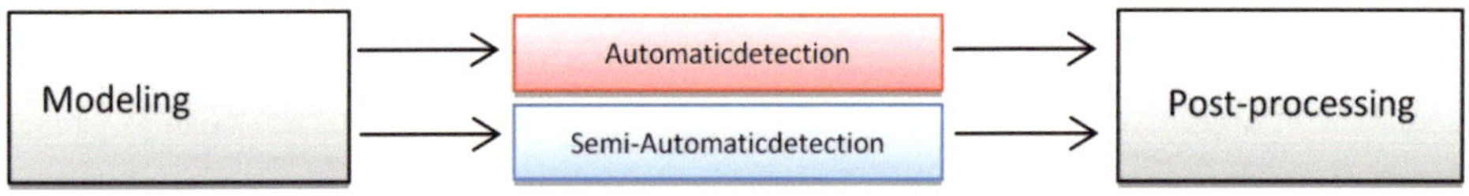

Figure 9. The steps of the proposed framework.

3.2.1. Modeling

The modeling process is an offline task. It is composed of three steps:

i. *Geometric model construction:* In this step, we build a vertebra mean model representing the average shape corresponding to a set of 25 vertebrae. The contour used to create this mean shape was extracted manually. the resulting model is shown in Figure 2(a)

ii. *Gradient computation and edge detection:* We use the canny operator to extract the edge of the vertebrae mean model. Canny operator was proposed in 1986 [19]. It is widely used in image processing and provides an accurate result for edge detection.

Within this operator, the image is first smoothed to reduce the noise. This step is realized by convolving the image with the kernel of Gaussian filter defined by equation (3):

$$G(x, y)=\frac{1}{\sqrt{2\pi\sigma^2}}e^{-(x^2+y^2)/2\sigma^2} \tag{3}$$

The gradient of each pixel in the smoothed image is computed by applying the Sobel-operator. The approximation is performed in horizontal and vertical directions by applying the two masks shown in equation (4).

$$G_x=\begin{bmatrix}-1 & 0 & 1\\ -2 & 0 & 2\\ -1 & 0 & 1\end{bmatrix} G_y=\begin{bmatrix}-1 & -2 & -1\\ 0 & 0 & 0\\ 1 & 2 & 1\end{bmatrix} \tag{4}$$

Then, the direction of the edges is determined by the equation (5).

$$\varphi=\arctan\left(\frac{G_x}{G_y}\right) \tag{5}$$

The next step is non-maximum suppression. Only the local maxima in the gradient image are preserved. Finally, an edge tracking by hysteresis is used, where high and low threshold are defined to make a filter for pixels of the last image.

The canny edge detection result is shown in Figure 2(b).

http://dx.doi.org/10.5772/50476

iii. *R-Table construction:* This offline phase of the GHT consists of calculating the template shape of the vertebra, constructed using information about position and direction of edge points computed in the last step.

Assuming that n denotes the number of model edge point $p_i(x_i, y_i)(i=1\ldots n)$ and φ_i its corresponding gradient. the refrence point$\vec{c}=(c_x, c_y)$is calculated by the equation (6):

$$\vec{c}=\frac{1}{n}\sum \vec{p}_i \tag{6}$$

The R-table is then constructed by analysing all the boundry points of the model shape. For each point p_i, we compute the distance r_i and $\beta_i$the angle between the horizontal direction and the reference point c as shown ine equation (7) and (8).

$$r_i=\sqrt{(x_c - x_i)^2 + (y_c - y_i)^2} \tag{7}$$

$$\beta_i=artan\left(\frac{y_i - y_c}{x_i - x_c}\right) \tag{8}$$

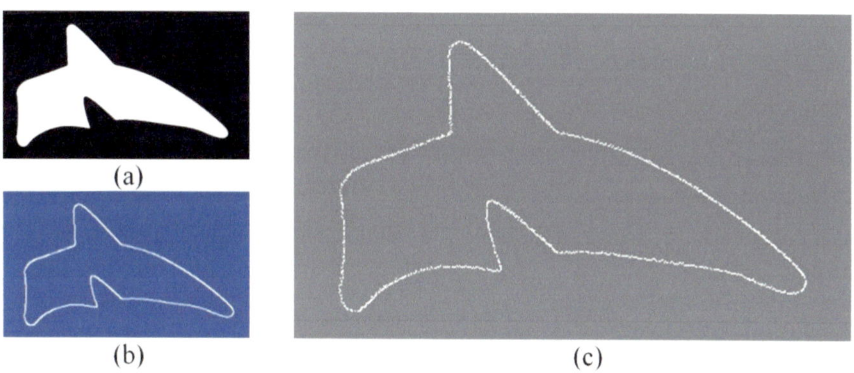

Figure 10. The modelling process results (a) Vertebra mean model, (b) Edge detection result, (c) the template shape constructed from the R-Table.

Therefore, the R-table allows to recompute the center point position, using edge points and the gradient information, equation (9).

$$c_x = x + rcos(\beta),\ c_y = y + r\sin(\beta) \tag{9}$$

The different parameters of the modified Hough transform are presented in Figure11.

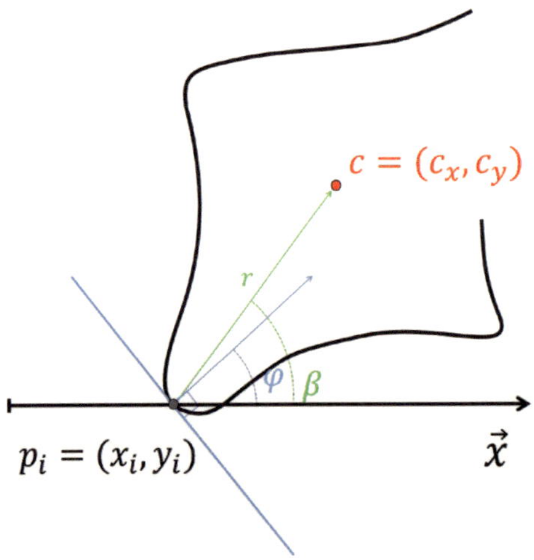

Figure 11. The GHT parameters corresponding to a model edge point.

The R-table construction algorithm can be expressed as follow (Listing 1):

1. Create the R-table.
2. For each edge point p_i, do:
   a. Compute the gradient direction φ
   b. Calculate r_i
   c. Calculate β_i
3. Increment r_i and β_i as a function of φ
4. End

Listing 1. Pre-processing steps used to create the R-table

Figure 10(c) shows the vertebra construction using only information stored in the R-Table.

3.2.2. *Potential vertebrae centers detection*

For the vertebrae detection we propose two alternative approaches, Automatic and semi-automatic detection. We make a preliminary pre-processing step based on histogram equalization to enhance X-ray images. Next, we use the Canny and Sobel operators for edge detection and gradient computation. Then, we perform GHT process based on the R-table calculated at offline training.

a. Pre-processing

- *Contrast-Limited Adaptive Histogram Equalization:*This step aims to prepare the X-ray images to edge detection by using the Contrast-Limited Adaptive Histogram Equalization (CLAHE) [3] technique used to improve the image contrast. It computes first different local histograms corresponding to each part of the image, and uses them to change the contrast of distinct regions of the image. This method is well known by limiting noise amplification. The result of this step is shown in Figure 13(b).

- *Gradient computation and edge detection:*In this step, we repeat the same process described in the model construction. Therefore, edge detection with Canny filter is applied to the improved image, and sobel operator is performed in –x and –y directions. The result of the edge detection is showen in figure 13(c).

b. Region of interest selection

We made two alternative approaches of our selection of Region of Interest (ROI). The different versions of ROI selection are presented in Figure 12.

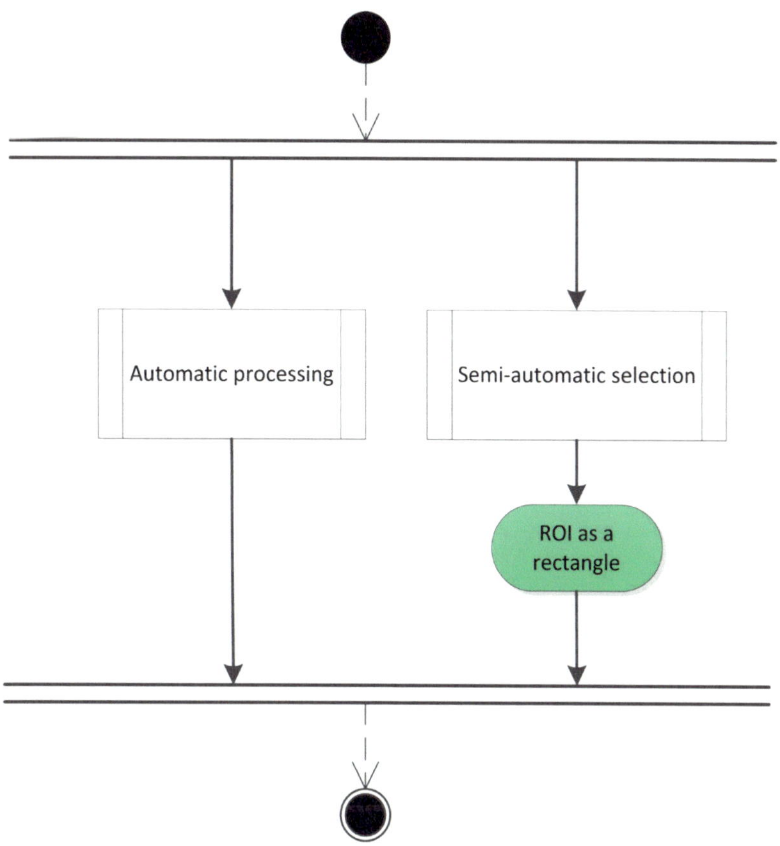

Figure 12. The two proposed processing of ROI selection.

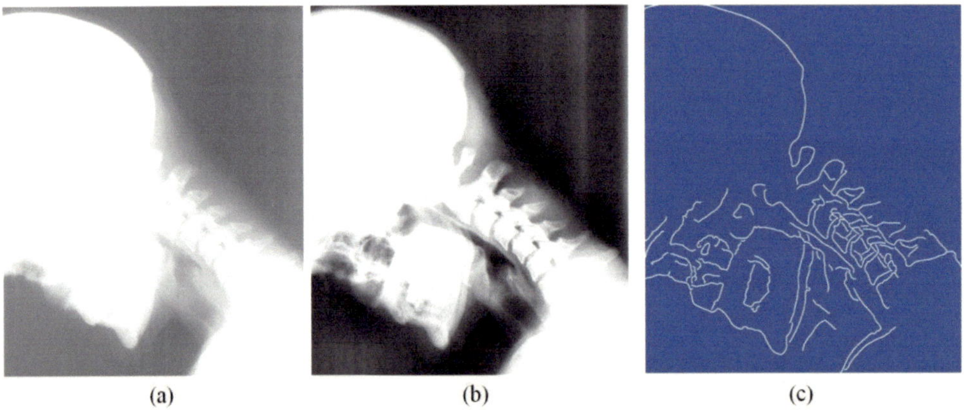

Figure 13. The proposed edge detection approach in case of cervical vertebrae (a)the original X-ray image, (b) the improved image, (c) The Canny edge detection result.

- *Automatic:* This algorithm travel through the image without any human action. Noises are observed in the final results.
- *Semi-automatic:* Two points are placed to make a sub-image covering the area of cervical vertebrae. The figure 14 shows the result selection

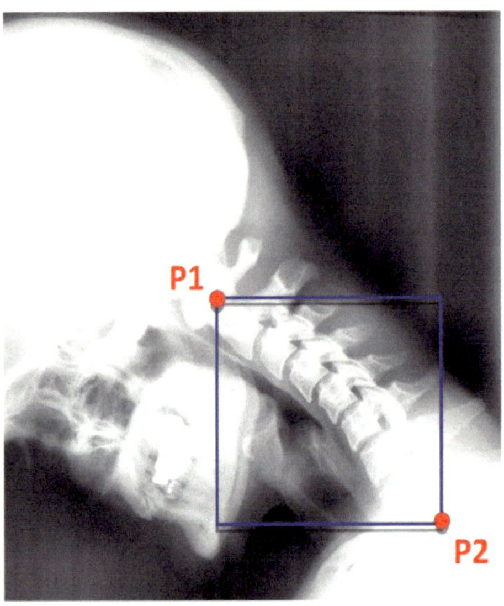

Figure 14. Semi-automatic ROI selection.

c. *Accumulator construction:*This step represents the core of the Generalized Hough Transform detection. It aims to determine the position of the center points of vertebrae in the input X-ray image by using the information stored in the R-table.

http://dx.doi.org/10.5772/50476

In practice, each point from the edge detection results, figure 13(c), votes for different possible centers. The selection is based on the gradient direction of the target point and its corresponding information in the R-table. These votes are stored in an accumulator.

The proposed model may be not easily matched. For this reason, we add a new parameter to make a range of scale to enhance the detection process. Therefore, a voted point can be expressed by its two coordinates x and y:

$$\begin{bmatrix} a \\ b \end{bmatrix} = \begin{bmatrix} x_i \\ y_i \end{bmatrix} + s * r_{\varphi}^{j} \begin{bmatrix} \text{coscos}\left(\beta_{\varphi}^{j}\right) \\ \text{sinsin}\left(\beta_{\varphi}^{j}\right) \end{bmatrix} \tag{10}$$

Wheresis the scale, $(r_{\varphi}^{j}, \beta_{\varphi}^{j})$ the parameters obtained in (5) and (6) corresponding to φ value in the R-table. Listing 2 summarize the detection algorithm.

1. Find all edge detection points
2. For each feature point (x_i, y_i)
   a. Compute the gradient direction φ
   b. For each $(r_{\varphi}^{j}, \beta_{\varphi}^{j})$ indexed under φ in the R-table
      - For each scale s, compute the candidate center (a, b)
      - Increment (a, b) in the accumulator.
3. Potential centers are given by local maxima in the accumulator

Listing 2. Detection algorithm of the Generalized Hough transform method.

3.2.3. Post-processing analysis:

For the post processing analysis we propose a new powerful issue in order to consider in a more global way the results given by the GHT voting procedure. This process is composed of four steps:

a. *Image grid cost:* We divide the image area into small squares which sizes are depending of the image resolution. We attribute to each of these areas a value determined by a cost function at first depending only of the number of votes. Each square vote for a unique point computed as a mean of all inside points

   This method gives some good results on quality radiographies but quickly reach its limitations by detecting mainly false positive. That is why, in addition to this first detection process, we introduce a new cost function, in order to eliminate the false positives.

b. *Top voted:* Based on the top three voted centers from the last step, we keep only the points that are in a specific distance computed in an offline process based on experimentations,area of the first and third quadrant in figure 15. Then, we repeat the same process for the selected point. This technique respects the inclination of the neck.

c. *Linear regression fitting:*Among the set of possible vertebrae extracted, the good ones are those forming a line, globally orthogonal to the orientation of the considered vertebra. We apply a simple linear regression based on a processing selection of top voted point from the accumulator.

The objective of this step is to select the effectively voted points$(x,\ y)$ based on the straight line equation (11).

$$\begin{cases} y = ax + b \\ a = \dfrac{S_{xy}}{S_{xx}} \\ b = \bar{y} - a\bar{x} \end{cases} \tag{11}$$

Where $S_{xy} = \sum (x_i - \bar{x})(y_i - \bar{y})$

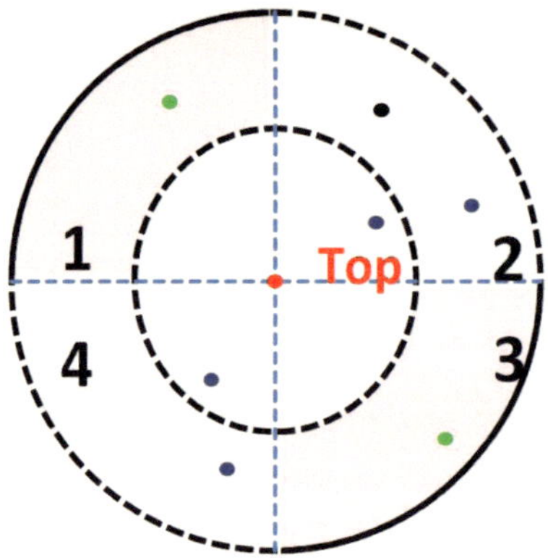

Figure 15. Region of selection around the top voted point in color.

d. *Adaptive distance filter:* An adaptive filter is finally applied to the result of the linear regression fitting step. This task aims to check the distance between selected points. Based on these distance, we compute the average distance between vertebrae centers. This enables us to eliminate false centers (with a distance higher or smaller than the average distance).

3.3. Experiments and results

Experimentations have been conducted using a set of 40 digitized X-ray films. These images presenting cervical spine region (Figure 13(a)) are obtained from the National Health and Nutrition Examination Surveys database NHANES II.

These experimentations are focused on the detection of the cervical vertebrae C3 to C7 (Figure 16). Indeed, our input images contain a total of 200 (40x5) vertebrae. We notice that the mean model was build using a set of 25 cervical vertebrae (Figure10(a)).

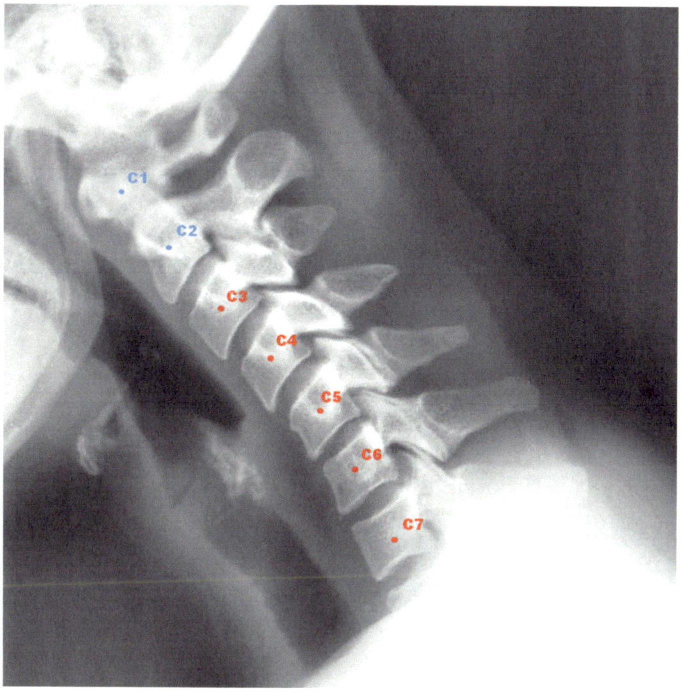

Figure 16. Cervical vertebra C1 to C7.

Figure17 and Figure 18 shows the obtained results by using thetwo proposed approaches in case of four X-ray images. These results enabled a global accuracy of 64,5% with automatic detection and 89% with the semi-automatic detection on the 200 vertebrae investigated as shown in Table 2. Notice that the C7 vertebra is detected with a rate of 32,5% and 60% with the two techniques which is lower than the mean accuracy. This is due to the edge detection step which does not detect efficiently this vertebra. The noise surrounding this cervical area makes this detection more difficult. We note 35,5% of false detection in the automatic technique.

Vertebrae type	*Detection rate*			
	Automatic		*Semi-automatic*	
	True	*False*	*True*	*False*
C3	70,0%	35,5%	97,5%	0%
C4	77,5%		95,0%	
C5	65,0%		95,0%	
C6	77,5%		97,5%	
C7	32,5%		60,0%	
Global	64,5%		89,0%	

Table 2. Accuracy recognition.

We note also that the edge detection and gradient computation steps depend on the contrast level of the input images. The use of CLAHE method allowed to achieve an efficient gradient computation, and hence enhanced the edge extraction.

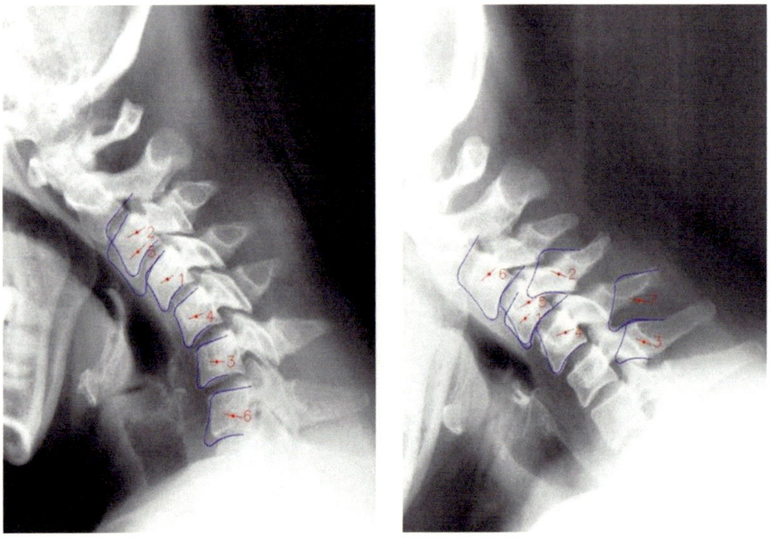

(a) (b)

Figure 17. Final result detection of C3 to C7 cervical vertebrae with the automaticapproach (a) Five detection and one false positive, (b)Three detections and four false positives.

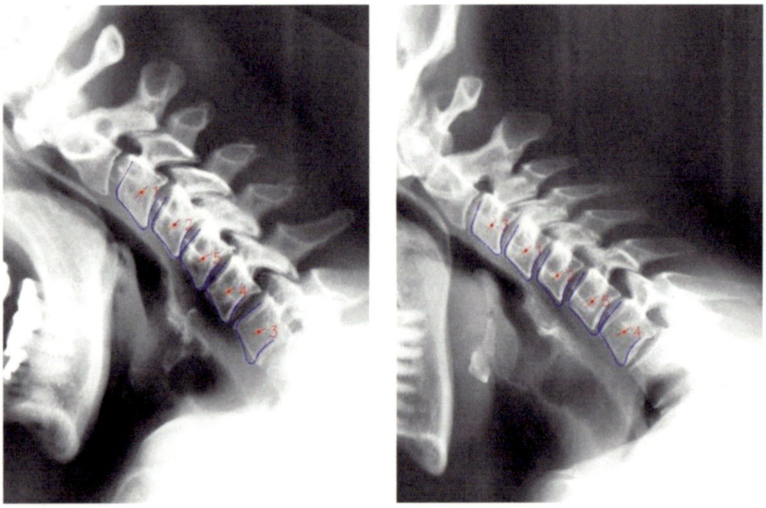

Figure 18. Final result detection of C3 to C7 cervical vertebrae with the semi-automatic approach for two cases.

http://dx.doi.org/10.5772/50476

4. Conclusion

In this chapter we have proposed a set of medical images detection and segmentation methods applied to vertebrae identification. We have first introduced a pre-processing operation that consists on defining a global polygonal region for each vertebra. This pre-treatment was used as a first step of three semi-automatic segmentation methods allowing to locate vertebrae positions and contours. These methods are based on automatic corner detection, polar signature and face detection. We have also proposed another semi-automatic segmentation approach based on the widely used active shape model theory.

On the other hand we have proposed using the Generalized Hough Transform –GHT– to perform semi-automatic and automatic vertebrae detection methods. The GHT technique is a powerful method for object recognition. It has a lot of advantages, like robustness under partial or slightly deformed shapes, tolerance to noise, and the ability to find multiple occurrences of a shape during the same processing task. In the GHT method, the model shape is represented by an R-table, which presents a discrete lookup table based on its edge information. The references points corresponding to the shapes to be detected are deduced from an accumulator containing an array of votes related to each point on the initial boundary shape. The points corresponding to highest number of votes represent the references point candidate and indicate the position of the model in the image. In addition to this first detection process, we introduced a new cost function that consisted on a grid based voting procedure. We applied also a post-processing analysis based on a linear regression fitting and an adaptive distance filter. As result, the proposed methods give promising detection rate for a large set of X-ray images. For our future works we plan to make an optimization of the GHT transform to increase the vertebrae detection accuracy and also computing time.

Author details

Mohammed Benjelloun, Saïd Mahmoudi and Mohamed Amine Larhmam

*Address all correspondence to: said.mahmoudi@umons.ac.be

Department of Computer Science, Faculty of Engineering University of Mons, Belgium

References

[1] Pham, D. L., Xu, C., & Prince, J. L. (2000). Current methods in medical image segmentation. *Annual Review of Bimedical Engineering*, 2, 315-337.

[2] Sethian, J. A. (1999). *Level Set Methods and Fast Marching Methods*, Cambridge University Press.

[3] Tan, S., Yao, J., Ward, M. M., Yao, L., & Summers, R. M. (2006). Level set based vertebra segmentation for the evaluation of ankylosing spondylitis. *Progress in biomedical optics and imaging*, 7(1, 30), 12-24.

[4] Kass, M., Witkin, A., & Terzopoulos, D. (1988). Snakes: Active contour models. *International Journal of Computer Vision*, 1(4), 321-331.

[5] Lobregt, S., & Viergever, M. (1995). A discrete dynamic contour model. *IEEE Transactions on Medical Imaging*, 14(1), 12-24.

[6] Benjelloun, M., & Mahmoudi, S. (2008). X-ray image segmentation for vertebral mobility analysis. *International Journal of Computer Assisted Radiology and Surgery*, 2(6), 371-383.

[7] Mc Inerney, T., & Terzopoulos, D. (1996). Deformable models in medical image analysis: A survey. *Medical Image Analysis*, 1(2), 91-108.

[8] Benjelloun, M., & Mahmoudi, S. (2009). Spine Localization in X-ray Images Using Interest Point Detection. Journal of Digital Imaging, juin http://dx.doi.org/10.1007/s10278-007-9099-3 , 22(3), 309-318.

[9] Keren, D. (2004). Topologically Faithful Fitting of Simple Closed Curves. *IEEE Transactions on PAMI*, 26(1).

[10] Benjelloun, M., Tellez, H. J., Oliva, R., & Prevot, . (2007, December 31). Edge Closing of Synthetic and Real Images using Polynomial Fitting. *JCIT: Journal of Convergence Information Technology*, 2(4), 8-19, 1975-9320.

[11] Benjelloun, M., & Mahmoudi, S. (2007). Mobility Estimation and Analysis in Medical X-ray Images Using Corners and Faces Contours Detection. International Machine Vision and Image Processing Conference IMVIP 5th-7th September, Maynooth (NUIM) Dublin, Ireland 978-0-7695-2887-8 , 01, 106-116.

[12] Cootes, T. F., Hill, A., Taylor, C. J., & Haslam, J. (1994). Use of active shape models for locating structures in medical images. *Image and Vision Computing*, 12(6), 355-365.

[13] Cootes, T. F., Taylor, C. J., Cooper, D. H., & Graham, J. (1995). Active shape models: Their training and application. *Computer Vision and Image Understanding*, 61(1), 38-59.

[14] Benjelloun, M., Mahmoudi, S., & Lecron, F. (2010, 20-23 January, 2010). Paper presented at 3rdInternational Conference on Bio-inspired Systems and Signal Processing, Valencia, Spain. *A New Semi-Automatic Approch for X-Ray Cervical Images Segmentation Using Active Shape Model*, BIOSIGNALS, 501-506.

[15] Tezmol, H., Sari-Sarraf, S., Mitra, A., Gururajan, R., & Long, . (2002). Customized Hough Transform for Robust Segmentation of Cervical Vertebrae from X-Ray Images. Paper presented at Fifth IEEE Southwest Symposium on Image Analysis and Interpretation. *Image Analysis and Interpretation, IEEE Southwest Symposium on*, 0224.

[16] Mahmoudi, S., & Benjelloun, M. (2007). A New Approach for Cervical Vertebrae Segmentation. Lecture Notes in Computer Science. 4756, *Progress in Pattern Recognition, Image Analysis and Applications*, 753-762.

[17] Chevrefils, C., Chériet, F., & Grimard, F. G. (2007). Watershed segmentation of intervertebral disk and spinal canal from MRI images. *In: Kamel M, ed. Image Analysis and Recognition: Lecture Notes in Computer Science*, Berlin, Germany, Springer, 1017-27.

[18] Ballard, D. H. (1981). Generalizing the Hough transform to detect arbitrary Shapes. *Pattern Recogn.*, 13(2), 111-122.

[19] Canny, J. (1986). A computational approach to edge detection. *IEEE Transactions on Pattern Analysis and Machine Intelligence*, 8(6).

[20] Pizer, S. M., Amburn, E. P., Austin, J. D., et al. (1987). Adaptive histogram equalization and its variations. *Computer Vision, Graphics, and Image Processing*, 39(3), 355-368.

Chapter 2

Image Segmentation and Time Series Clustering Based on Spatial and Temporal ARMA Processes

Ronny Vallejos and Silvia Ojeda

Additional information is available at the end of the chapter

http://dx.doi.org/10.5772/50513

1. Introduction

During the past decades, image segmentation and edge detection have been two important and challenging topics. The main idea is to produce a partition of an image such that each category or region is homogeneous with respect to some measures. The processed image can be useful for posterior image processing treatments.

Spatial autoregressive moving average (ARMA) processes have been extensively used in several applications in image/signal processing. In particular, these models have been used for image segmentation, edge detection and image filtering. Image restoration algorithms based on robust estimation of a two-dimensional process have been developed (Kashyap & Eom 1988). Also the two-dimensional autoregressive model has been used to perform unsupervised texture segmentation (Cariou & Chehdi, 2008). Generalizations of the previous algorithms using the generalized M estimators to deal with the effect caused by additive contamination was also addressed (Allende et al., 2001). Later on, robust autocovariance (RA) estimators for two dimensional autoregresive (AR-2D) processes were introduced (Ojeda, 2002). Several theoretical contributions have been suggested in the literature, including the asymptotic properties of a nearly unstable sequence of stationary spatial autoregressive processes (Baran et al., 2004). Other contributions and applications of spatial ARMA processes have been considered in many publications (Basu & Reinsel, 1993, Bustos 2009a, Francos & Friendlaner1998, Guyon 1982, Ho 2011, Illig & Truong-Van 2006, Martin1996, Vallejos & Mardesic 2004).

A new approach to perform image segmentation based on the estimation of AR-2D processes has been recently suggested (Ojeda 2010). First an image is locally modeled using a spatial autoregressive model for the image intensity. Then the residual autoregressive image is computed. This resulting image possesses interesting texture features. The borders and edges are highlighted, suggesting that the algorithm can be used for border detection. Experimental results with real images clarify how the algorithm works in practice. A robust version of the algorithm was also proposed, to be used when the original image is contaminated with additive outliers. Applications in the context of image inpainting were also offered.

Another concern that has been pointed out in the context of spatial statistics is the development of coefficients to compare two spatial processes. Coefficients that take into account the spatial association between two processes have been proposed in the literature. (Tjostheim, 1978) suggested a nonparametric coefficient to assess the spatial association between two spatial variables. Later on, (Clifford et al. 1989) proposed an hypothesis testing procedure to study the spatial dependence between two spatial sequences. Rukhin & Vallejos (2008) studied asymptotic properties of the codispersion coefficient first introduced by Matheron(1965). The performance and impact of this coefficient to quantify the spatial association between two images is currently under study Ojeda et al. (2012). An adaptation of this coefficient to time series analysis was studied in Vallejos (2008).

In the context of clustering time series Chouakria & Nagabhushan (2007) proposed a distance measure that is a function of the codispersion coefficient. This measure includes the correlation behavior and the proximity of two time series. They proposed to combine these distances in a multiplicative way, introducing a tuning constant controlling the weight of each quantity in the final product. This makes the measure flexible to model sequences with different behaviors, comparing them in terms of both correlation and dissimilarity between the values of the series.

The structure of this chapter consist in two parts. In the first part we review some theoretical aspects of the spatial ARMA processes. Then the algorithm suggested by Ojeda(2010), its limitations and advantages are briefly described. In order to propose a more efficient algorithm new variants of this algorithm are suggested specially to address the problem of determining the most convenient (in terms of the quality of the segmentation) prediction window of unilateral AR-2D processes. The computation of the distance between the filtered images and the original one will be done by using the codispersion coefficient and other image quality measures (Wang and Bovik 2002). Examples with real images will highlight the features of the modified algorithm. In the second part, the codispersion coefficient previously used to measure the closeness between images is utilized in a distance measure to perform cluster analysis of time series. The distance measure introduced in Chouakria & Nagabhushan (2007) is generalized in the sense that considers an arbitrary lag h that allows us to capture a higher serial correlation of two temporal or spatial sequences. Examples and numerical studies are presented to explore our proposal in several different scenarios. We explore the performance of hierarchical methods to classify correlated sequences when the proposed proximity measure is used, employing the Monte Carlo simulation. An application is discussed for time series measuring the Normalized Difference Vegetation Index (NDVI) in four locations of Argentina. The clusters formed using hierarchical classification techniques with the proposed distance measure preserve the geographical location where the series were obtained, providing information that is unavailable when using hierarchical methods with conventional distance measures.

2. Image Segmentation Through Estimation of Spatial ARMA Processes

2.1. The Spatial ARMA Processes

Spatial ARMA processes have been studied in the context of random fields indexed over $\mathbb{Z}^d$, $d \geq 2$, where $\mathbb{Z}^d$ is endowed with the usual partial order. That is, for $s=(s_1, s_2, \ldots, s_d)$, $u=(u_1, u_2, \ldots, u_d)$ in $\mathbb{Z}^d$, $s \leq u$ if for $i=1, 2, \ldots, d$, $s_i \leq u_i$ For $a, b \in \mathbb{Z}^d$, such that $a \leq b$ and $a \neq b$, we define $S[a, b]=\{x \in \mathbb{Z}^d \mid a \leq x \leq b\}$ and $S\langle a, b]=S[a, b] \setminus \{a\}$.

A random field $(X_s)_{s \in \mathbb{Z}^d}$ is said to be a spatial ARMA(p, q) with parameters $p, q \in \mathbb{Z}^d$ if it is weakly stationary and satisfies the equation

$$X_s - \sum_{j \in S\langle 0,p]} \phi_j X_{s-j} = \varepsilon_t + \sum_{k \in S\langle 0,q]} \theta_j \varepsilon_{s-j}, \tag{1}$$

where $(\phi_j)_{j \in S\langle 0,p]}$ and $(\varepsilon_j)_{k \in S\langle 0,q]}$, respectively, denote the autoregressive and moving average parameters with $\phi_0 = \theta_0 = 1$, and $(\varepsilon_s)_{s \in \mathbb{Z}^d}$ denotes a sequence of independent and identically distributed centered random variables with variance σ^2. Notice that if $p=0$, the sum over $S\langle 0, p]$ is supposed to be zero, and the process is called a spatial moving average MA (q) random field. Similarly, if $q=0$, the process is called a spatial autoregressive AR(p) random field. The ARMA random field is labeled as causal if it has the following unilateral representation.

$$X_s = \sum_{[j \in S\ 0,\infty]} \psi_j \varepsilon_{s-j}$$

with $\sum_j |\phi_j| < \infty$. Similar to the time series case, there are conditions on the (AR or MA) polynomials that ensure stationarity and invertibility, respectively. Let $\Phi(z) = 1 - \sum_{j \in S\langle 0,p]} \phi_j z^j$ and $\Theta(z) = 1 - \sum_{j \in S\langle 0,q]} \theta_j z^j$, where $z=(z_1, z_2, \ldots, z_d)$ and $z^j = z_1^{j_1} z_2^{j_2} \ldots z_d^{j_d}$. A sufficient condition for the random field to be causal is that the AR polynomial $\Phi(z)$ has no zeros in the closure of the open disc D^d in $\mathbb{C}^d$. For example, if $d=2$, the process is causal if $\Phi(z_1, z_2)$ is not zero for any z_1 and z_2 that simultaneously satisfy $|z_1| < 1$ and $|z_2| < 1$ (Jain et al., 1999).

Applications of spatial ARMA processes have been developed, including analysis of yield trials in the context of incomplete block designs (Cullis & Glesson 1991, Grondona et al. 1996) and the study of spatial unilateral first-order ARMA model (Basu & Reinsel, 1993). Other theoretical extensions of time series and spatial ARMA models can be found in (Baran et al., 2004, Bustos et al., 2009b, Gaetan & Guyon 2010, Choi 2000, Genton & Koul 2008, Guo 1998, Vallejos and Garccía-Donato 2006).

2.2. An Image Segmentation Algorithm

In this section, we describe an image segmentation algorithm that is based on a previous fitting of spatial autoregressive models to an image. This fitted image is constructed by dividing the original image into squared sub-images (e.g.,8×8) and then fitting a spatial autoregressive model to each sub-image (i.e., block). Then, we generate a sub-image from each local fitted model, preserving intensities on the boundary to smooth the edges between blocks. The final fitted image is yielded by putting together all generated sub-images.

Let$Z = Z_{m,n}, 0 \le m \le M-1 \quad, 0 \le n \le N-1$, be the original image, and let$X = X_{m,n}$, $0 \le m \le M-1$, $0 \le n \le N-1$, where for all$0 \le m \le M-1, 0 \le n \le N-1$,$X_{m,n} = Z_{m,n} - \overline{Z}$, and $\overline{Z}$is the mean of$Z$. Let $4 \le k \le \min(M, N)$and consider the rearrange images

$Z = Z_{m,n}$,

$X = X_{m,n}$,

where$0 \le m \le M' - 1, 0 \le n \le N' - 1$, $M' = \left[\frac{M-1}{k-1}\right](k-1)+1, N' = \left[\frac{N-1}{k-1}\right](k-1)+1$. For all $i_b = 1, \cdots, \left[\frac{M-1}{k-1}\right]$and for all $j_b = 1, \cdots, \left[\frac{N-1}{k-1}\right]$the $(k-1)\times(k-1)$block $(i_b, j_b)$of the image X is defined as

$B_X(i_b, j_b) = X_{r,s}$,

where $(k-1)(i_b-1)+1 \le r \le (k-1)i_band(k-1)(j_b-1)+1 \le s \le (k-1)j_b$. Then, the approximated image $\hat{X}$ of X is provided by Algorithm 1.

Algorithm 1.

For each block $B_X(i_b, j_b)$

1. Compute estimators$\hat{\phi}_1(i_b, j_b)$, $\hat{\phi}_2(i_b, j_b)$of ϕ_1 and $\phi_2$corresponding to the block $B_X(i_b, j_b)$extended to:

$B'_X(i_b, j_b) = X_{r,s}$,

where$(k-1)(i_b-1) \le r \le (k-1)i_b$,$(k-1)(j_b-1) \le s \le (k-1)j_b$.

2. Let $\hat{X}$ be defined on the block $B_X(i_b, j_b)$by

$\hat{X}_{r,s} = \hat{\phi}_1(i_b, j_b) X_{r-1,s} + \hat{\phi}_2(i_b, j_b) X_{r,s-1}$

where $(k-1)(i_b-1)+1 \le r \le (k-1)i_b$and $(k-1)(j_b-1)+1 \le s \le (k-1)j_b$.

Then the approximated image $\hat{Z}$of the original image $Z$is:

$\hat{Z}_{m,n} = \hat{X}_{m,n} + \overline{Z}, \quad 0 \le m \le M'-1, \ 0 \le n \le N'-1.$

The image segmentation algorithm we describe below is supported by a widely known notion in regression analysis. If a fitted image very well represents the patterns on the original image, then the residual image (i.e., the fitted image minus the observed image) will not contain useful information about the original patterns because the model already explains the features that are present in the original image. On the contrary, if the model does not well represent the patterns that are present in the original image, then the residual image will contain useful information that has not been explained by the model. Thus, to implement an algorithm based on these notions, we must characterize which patterns are present in the residual image when the fitted image is not a good representation of the original one, and we must develop a technique to produce a fitting that is satisfactory in terms of segmentation but not a very good estimation in that the residual image still contains valuable information. (Ojeda et al. 2010) investigated these concerns and, based on several numerical experiments with images, determined that the residual image associated with a good local fitting is in fact poor in terms of structure (i.e., it is very similar to a white noise). However, when the fitted image is poor in terms of estimation, the residual image is useful for highlighting the boundaries and edges of the original image. Moreover, a bad fitting is related to the size of the block (or window) used in Algorithm 1. The best performance is attained for the maximum block size, which would be the size of the original image. The image segmentation algorithm introduced by (Ojeda et al. 2010) can be summarized as follows.

Algorithm 2.

1. Use Algorithm 1 to generate an approximated image $\hat{Z}$of Z.

2. Compute the residual autoregressive image given by $Z-\hat{Z}$

Example 1. We present examples with real images to illustrate the performance of Algorithms 1 and 2. These images were taken from the database http://sipi.usc.edu/database. Figure 1(a) shows an original image of size512×512 (aerial), and Figure 1(b) shows the image generated by Algorithm 1 when a moving window of size $512\times512$is used to define an AR-2D process on the plane. It is not possible to visualize the differences between the original and fitted images. However, the residual image (Fig 1(c)) shows patterns that the model is not able to capture. Basically, the AR-2D model does not capture the changes in the texture produced by lines, borders and object boundaries. These features are contained in the residual image produced by Algorithm 2 such that the good performance of Algorithm 2 is associated with a moderate fitting of the AR-2D model. Another image (peepers) was processed by Algorithm 2 to show the effect of the size of the moving window. Figure 2(b) shows the segmentation produced by Algorithm 2 using a moving window of size 128×128. Another segmentation with a moving of size $512\times512$is shown in Figure 2. In both cases, the segmentations highlight the borders and boundaries present in the original image.

2.3. Improving the Segmentation Algorithm

In all experiments carried out in (Ojeda et al., 2010) and (Quintana et al., 2011), Algorithm 1 was implemented using the same prediction window for the AR-2D process, which contains only two elements belonging to a strongly causal region on the plane. Here, we consider other prediction windows to observe the effect on the performance of Algorithm 2. A description

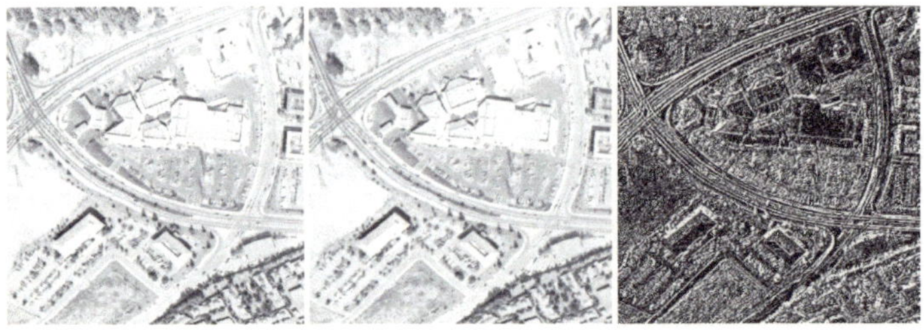

(a) Original image (aerial) (b) Image generated by Algorithm 1 (c) Residual image generated by Algorithm 2

Figure 1. Images generated by Algorithms 1 and 2.

(a) Original image (peppers) (b) Residual image (c) Residual image

Figure 2. (b)-(c) Images generated by Algorithm 2 with prediction windows of $128\times128$and 512×512respectively.

of the most commonly used prediction windows in statistical image processing is in Bustos et al., (2009a). A brief description of the strongly causal prediction windows is given below.

For all $(m, n)\in\mathbb{Z}^2$, a strongly causal region at (m, n) is defined as

$$S(m, n)=\{(k, l)\in\mathbb{Z}^2 : k\leq m, l\leq n)\}-\{(m, n)\} \tag{2}$$

For a given $M\in\mathbb{N}$, a strongly causal prediction window is

$$W=\{(k, l)\in s(m, n) : m-M\leq k\leq m, n-M\leq l\leq n\}. \tag{3}$$

In particular, if$M=1$, then a strongly causal prediction window containing three elements is

$$W_1=\{(k, l)\in s(m, n) : m-1\leq k\leq m, n-1\leq l\leq n\} \tag{4}$$

The set W_1 is shown in Figure 3 (b). Similarly, strongly causal prediction windows can be defined by considering not only the top left quadrant on the plane $\mathbb{Z}^2$.The definition of such sets generates the prediction windows W_2, W_3, andW_4, as shown in Figure3(b). Algorithms

1 and 2 were implemented using the prediction windows W_1, W_2, W_3, and W_4, with two elements each (Figure 3(a)).

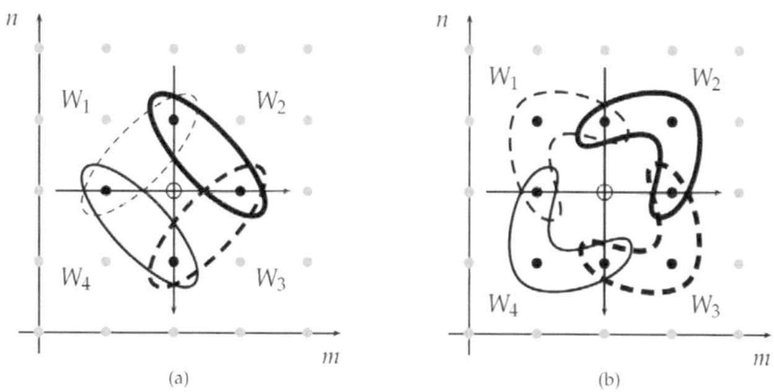

Figure 3. Strongly causal prediction windows.

Visually, the best segmentation for the aerial image is yielded by the prediction window W_2. The lines and edges are better highlighted in this segmentation (Figure 4(b)) than in the other segmentations. The dark regions are also stressed, which provides a more intense and brighter partition of the original features.

To gain insight on image quality measures, the fitted images produced by Algorithm 1 associated with the images shown in Figure 4(a) -(d) were compared aerially with the original image using three coefficients described in (Ojeda et al., 2012). These coefficients are briefly described below.

Consider two weakly stationary processes, $(X_s)_{s\in D}$ *and* $(Y_s)_{s\in D}$, $D\subset\mathbb{Z}^d$.For a given $h\in D$, the codispersion coefficient is defined as

$$\rho(h)=\frac{\gamma(h)}{\sqrt{V_X(h)V_Y(h)}}, \tag{5}$$

where $s,\ s+h\in D$, $\gamma(h)=\mathrm{E}[X(s+h)-X(s)][Y(s+h)-Y(s)]$, $V_X(h)=\mathrm{E}[X(s+h)-X(s)]^2$(and similarly for$\mathrm{V}_Y(h)$).

For $d=2$, the sample codispersion coefficient is defined by

$$\hat{\rho}(h)=\frac{\sum_{s,s+h\in D'}a_s b_s}{\sqrt{\hat{V}_X(h)\hat{V}_Y(h)}} \tag{6}$$

with$s=(s_1,\ s_2)$, $h=(h_1,\ h_2)$, $D'\subseteq D$, $\#(D')<\infty$, $a_s=X(s_1+h_1,\ s_2+h_2)-X(s_1,\ s_2)$, $b_s=Y(s_1+h_1,\ s_2+h_2)-Y(s_1,\ s_2)$, $\hat{V}_X(h)=\sum_{s,s+h\in D'}a_s^2$, and $\hat{V}_Y(h)=\sum_{s,s+h\in D'}b_s^2$.

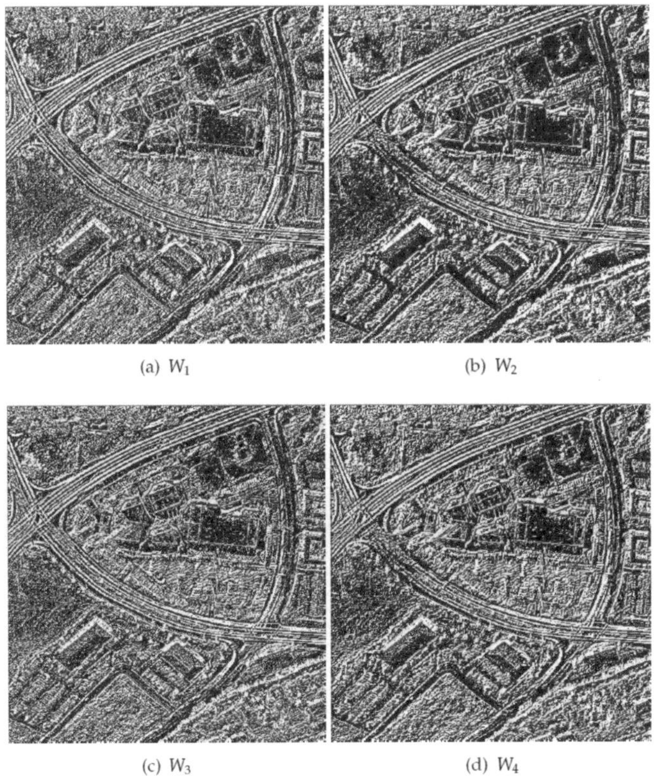

Figure 4. a)-(d) Images generated by Algorithm 2 with prediction windows $W_1 - W_4$respectively.

The index Q (Wang and Bovik, 2002) is

$$Q = \frac{4S_{XY}\overline{X}\,\overline{Y}}{(S_X^2 + S_Y^2)[\overline{X}^2 + \overline{Y}^2]} = \frac{S_{XY}}{S_X S_Y} \cdot \frac{2\overline{X}\,\overline{Y}}{\overline{X}^2 + \overline{Y}^2} \cdot \frac{2S_X S_Y}{S_X^2 + S_Y^2} = C \cdot M \cdot V, \tag{7}$$

where $\overline{X}$ is the mean of$(X_s)_{s\in D}$, $S_X$is the standard deviation of $(X_s)_{s\in D}$, and S_{XY} is the covariance between $(X_s)_{s\in D}$and $(Y_s)_{s\in D}$(and similarly for $\overline{Y}$andS_Y). The quantity $C = S_{XY} / S_X S_Y$models the linear correlation between $(X_s)_{s\in D}$ and$(Y_s)_{s\in D}$, $M = 2\overline{X}\,\overline{Y} / (\overline{X}^2 + \overline{Y}^2)$measures the similarity between the sample means (luminance) of $(X_s)_{s\in D}$and$(Y_s)_{s\in D}$, and $V = 2S_X S_Y / (S_X^2 + S_Y^2)$measures the similarity related to the contrast between the images. Coefficient Q is defined as a function of the correlation coefficient; hence, it is able to capture only the linear association between $(X_s)_{s\in D}$and$(Y_s)_{s\in D}$ It is unable to account for other types of relationships between these sequences, including the spatial association in a specific direction h. Ojeda et al. (2012) suggested by the CQindex, which is defined as:

$$CQ(h)=\hat{\rho}(h)\cdot M\cdot V, \tag{8}$$

where M and V are defined as in (7).

The correlation coefficient and the coefficients defined in (6), (7) and (8) were computed to compare the fitted images, which were generated with a prediction window with two elements and associated with the images shown in Figure 4(a) -(f), and the original images. The results are shown in Table 1. In all cases, the highest values of the image quality measures are attained for the image fitted using the prediction window W_2.This means that the residual image shown in Figure 4 (b) is the best segmentation yielded by Algorithm 2. The same

Coefficient	Original-Fitted(W_1)	Original-Fitted(W_2)	Original- Fitted(W_3)	Original-Fitted(W_4)
Correlation	0.8985	0.9400	0.8899	0.8953
Q	0.8968	0.9384	0.8882	0.8935
		$h=(0,1)$		
$\hat{\rho}(h)$	0.3341	0.6130	0.3954	0.4779
$CQ(h)$	0.3336	0.6120	0.3947	0.4770
		$h=(1,1)$		
$\hat{\rho}(h)$	0.5457	0.7072	0.5040	0.4645
$CQ(h)$	0.5447	0.7060	0.5030	0.4036
		$h=(1,0)$		
$\hat{\rho}(h)$	0.4740	0.6655	0.3681	0.4980
$CQ(h)$	0.4731	0.6644	0.3675	0.4970

Table 1. Image quality measures between the fitted and original (aerial) images related to the residual images shown in Figure 4.

experiment was carried out for the image shown in Figure 2(a). Table 2 summarizes the values of the image quality coefficients for the fitted images generated by Algorithm 2 with prediction windows W_1, W_2, W_3, and W_4. In this case, the best performance is for the fitted image

Coefficient	Original-Fitted(W_1)	Original-Fitted(W_2)	Original- Fitted(W_3)	Original-Fitted(W_4)
Correlation	0.9801	0.9848	0.9800	0.9855
Q	0.9801	0.9847	0.9800	0.9854
		$h=(0,1)$		
$\hat{\rho}(h)$	0.2294	0.5191	0.2366	0.5321
$CQ(h)$	0.2294	0.5191	0.5303	0.2366
		$h=(1,1)$		
$\hat{\rho}(h)$	0.5158	0.5862	0.5134	0.6030
$CQ(h)$	0.5158	0.5862	0.5134	0.6029
		$h=(1,0)$		
$\hat{\rho}(h)$	0.2537	0.5267	0.2420	0.5386
$CQ(h)$	0.2537	0.5267	0.2420	0.5386

Table 2. Image quality measures between the fitted and original (peppers) images.

generated with prediction window W_4.In general, the performance of Algorithm 2 depends on the choice of the prediction window. One way to choose the prediction window that yields the best segmentation is to maximize the association between the fitted and original images. Indeed, if we denote the original image by Z and the fitted image generated by Algorithm 1 with the prediction window W_i by $\hat{Z}_{W_i}$, then the prediction window that produces the best segmentation can be obtained by finding the maximum value of one of the quality measures (6), (7) or (8) between Z and Z_{W_i}. This criterion is summarized in the following algorithm.

Algorithm 3.

1. Use Algorithm 1 to generate the approximated images $\hat{Z}_{W_i}$ of Z, $i=1, 2, 3, 4$.

2. Compute an image quality index between Z and $\hat{Z}_{W_i}$ for all $i=1, 2, 3, 4$. Suppose that the maximum value for the image quality index is attained for $\hat{Z}_{W_j}$, $1 \le j \le 4$. Then, the best fitted image is $\hat{Z}_{W_j}$.

3. Compute the residual autoregressive image $Z-\hat{Z}_{W_j}$.

3. Clustering Time series

3.1. Measuring Closeness and Association Between Time Series

Let $x=(x_1, x_2, \ldots, x_p)$ and $y=(y_1, y_2, \ldots, y_q)$ be two time series. There are several conventional distance measures between time series. For example, if $p=q=n$, then the Euclidean distance between x and y is defined as $d_E(x, y)=\left(\sum_{i=1}^{n}(x_i-y_i)^2\right)^{1/2}$. As is evident, d_E ignores information about the dependence between x and y. The Minkowski distance is a generalization of the Euclidean distance, which is defined as

$$d_M(x, y)=\left(\sum_{i=1}^{n}(x_i-y_i)^q\right)^{1/q}, \tag{9}$$

where q is a positive integer. The Fréchet distance was introduced to measure the proximity between continuous curves. Let m be a natural number such that $m \le \min(p, q)$. Let M be the set of all mappings r between x and y such that r is a sequence of m pairs preserving the order

$r=((x_{a_1}, y_{b_1}), (x_{a_2}, y_{b_2}), \ldots, (x_{a_m}, y_{b_m}))$,

where $a_i \in \{1, 2, ..., p\}$, $b_j \in \{1, 2, ...q\}$ with $a_1=1$, $b_1=1$, $a_m=p$, $b_m=q$ and for $i \in \{1, 2, \ldots, m-1\}$, $a_{i+1}=(a_i$ or $a_i+1)$ and $b_{i+1}=(b_i$ or $b_i+1)$. Note that $|r|=\max_{i=1,2,\ldots,m}|x_{a_i}-y_{b_i}|$ is the mapping length representing the maximum span between two coupled observations. Thus, the Fréchet distance between the series x and y is given by

$$d_F(x, y)=\min_{r\in M}|r|=\min_{r\in M}\left(\max_{i=1,2,\ldots,m}|x_{a_i}-y_{b_i}|\right). \tag{10}$$

Dynamic time warping (DTW) is a variant of the Fréchet distance that considers mapping length as the sum of the spans of all coupled observations. That is, $\left| r \right| = \sum_{i=1,2,\ldots,m} \left| x_{a_i} - y_{b_i} \right|$.

Dynamic time warping is then defined as

$$d_{DTW}(x, y) = \min_{r \in M} \left| r \right| = \min_{r \in M} \sum_{i=1,2,\ldots,m} \left| x_{a_i} - y_{b_i} \right|. \tag{11}$$

The distances defined above are based on the proximity of the values $\left| x_{a_i} - y_{b_i} \right|$. However, these distances disregard both the temporal dependence between the sequences x and y and the correlation structure of each sequence.

Several distance measures that are functions of the correlation between two sequences ($Cor(x, y)$) have been suggested. For example, (Golay et al.,1998) proposed $d_{cc}(x, y) = \left(\frac{1 - Cor(x, y)}{1 + Cor(x, y)} \right)^{\beta}$ and $d_{cc}^2(x, y) = 2(1 - Cor(x, y))$,

where β is a parameter related to the fuzzy c-means classification algorithm (Macqueen, 1967). However, none of these measures takes into account the serial association between the sequences because the correlation coefficient is a crude measure of association. This approach requires the study of coefficients that are capable of capturing the spatial or serial correlation between two sequences.

3.2. The Codispersion Coefficient for Time Series

Consider two weakly stationary processes, $X = \{X_s : s \in D \subset \mathbb{Z}\}$ and $Y = \{Y_s : s \in D \subset \mathbb{Z}\}$, and let x and y be realizations of these processes as in Section 3.1. For $d = 1$, the estimator (6) becomes

$$\hat{\rho}(h) = \frac{\sum_{t \in N(h)} (x_{t+h} - x_t)(y_{t+h} - y_t)}{\sqrt{\sum_{t \in N(h)} (x_{t+h} - x_t)^2 \sum_{t \in N(h)} (y_{t+h} - y_t)^2}} \tag{12}$$

where $N(h) = \{t : t + h \in D\}$, $N = \left| N(h) \right|$ is the cardinality of $N(h)$, and sequences x and y are realizations of processes x and y, respectively. The coefficient $\hat{\rho}(h)$ is called the comovement coefficient when $h = 1$. Although $\hat{\rho}(h)$ is not the correlation coefficient, the codispersion coefficient shares a number of its standard properties. For example, $\hat{\rho}(h)$ is translation invariant, positive homogeneous, symmetric in its arguments, positive definite for a sequence and lagged versions of itself, and interpretable as the cosine of the angle between the vectors formed by the first difference of the sampled series. As in the case of classic correlation, a codispersion coefficient of $+1$ indicates that the compared functions or processes are rescaled or retranslated versions of one another. Similarly, a profile matched with its reflection across the time axis yields a codispersion of -1. The value $\hat{\rho}(h) = 0$ expresses that there is no monotonicity between $x$and $y$and that their growth rates are stochastically linearly independent. More details can be found in (Rukhin & Vallejos, 2008 , Vallejos, 2008).

3.3. Dissimilarity Index for Time Series

This coefficient involves a distance measure and a correlation-type measure that addresses both the correlation behavior and the proximity of two time series. The dissimilarity index depends on similarity behaviors, which should be specified in advance. The suggested dissimilarity index $D(x, y, h)$for the realizations $x$and $y$and $d=1$is given by

$$D(x, y, h)=f(\hat{\rho}(h))\cdot d(x, y), \tag{13}$$

where f is an adaptive tuning function, and $d(x, y)$is one of the conventional distances described in Section 3.1 that summarizes the closeness of sequences $x$and$y$. There are many possible ways to choose a function f. Here, we follow the guidelines given in (Chouakria & Nagabhushan, 2007), according to which $f$is considered an exponential adaptive tuning function given by

$$f_k(t)=\frac{2}{1+exp(kt)}, \tag{14}$$

where $k\geq 0$modulates the contributions of the proximity with respect to values and behavior. For example, when $|\hat{\rho}(1)|$ is large and $k=2$, the proximity with respect to behavior contributes 76.2% to$D$. The flexibility of Dallows us to choose $k$such that for highly dependent sequences, the correlation structure can have a large weight in (13).

Note that (13) is a generalization of the dissimilarity index introduced in Chouakria & Nagabhushan, (2007). The dissimilarity index (13) can capture high-order serial correlations between the sequences because the distance lag $h$is arbitrary, while Chouakria's index only captures the first-order correlation.

The dependence of (13) on $h$is crucial, and in some specific cases, $h$can be chosen using an optimal criterion. For example, for two AR(1) processes with parameters $\phi_1$andϕ_2, respectively, and a correlation structure between the errors (Rukhin & Vallejos,2008), it is possible to find ϕ_1, $\phi_2$such that $Var(\hat{\rho}(1))Var(\hat{\rho}(2))$.In other words, for those processes in which the asymptotic variance of the codispersion coefficient is known, we suggest setting the value of $h$to produce the minimum variance. That is,

$$\hat{h}=\underset{h}{\operatorname{argmin}}[Var(\hat{\rho}(h))]. \tag{15}$$

When the variance of the codispersion coefficient is difficult to compute, resampling methods can be use to estimate the variance of the sample codispersion coefficient (Politis & Romano, 1994, Vallejos, 2008).

In the next section, we present two simulation examples to illustrate the capabilities of the hierarchical methods using the distance measure (13) under the tuning function given by (14). All else being constant, the clusters produced using traditional distances are usually different from those yielded using the distance measure (13).

3.4. Simulations

In this example, we simulate observations from six first-order autoregressive models to illustrate the clustering produced by hierarchical methods when the sequences exhibit serial correlation. To generate the series, we consider the following models.

$$X_t^i = \phi_i X_{t-1}^i + \varepsilon_t^i, \qquad i = 1, 2, \ldots 6,$$

where $\forall\, i = 1, 2, \ldots, 6$, $X^i = \{X_t^i\}_{t\in\mathbb{Z}}$ define the $i-$model, and the sequence $\varepsilon^i = \{\varepsilon_t^i\}_{t\in\mathbb{Z}}$ is zero-mean white noise. Note that the sequences ε^1 and ε^2 have the covariance structure

$$Cov(\varepsilon_t^1, \varepsilon_s^2) = \begin{cases} \rho\sigma\tau, & s = t, \\ 0, & \text{otherwise}, \end{cases}$$

with $\sigma^2 = \tau^2 = 1$, and $\rho = 0.9$. The same covariance structure is assumed for ε_t^1 and ε_t^3, with $\sigma^2 = \tau^2 = 1$ and $\rho = 0.7$. ε^i, $i = 4, 5, 6$, are assumed to be white noise processes with variance 1 and are uncorrelated with all other error sequences. If $i, j \le 3$, the correlation structure between processes X^i and X^j, $i \ne j$, is not null due to the correlation structure between ε^i and ε^j. Instead, if $i, j \ge 4$, $i \ne j$, the correlation structure between processes X^i and X^j vanishes.

Two hundred observations were generated from each model for $\phi_1 = -0.5$, $\phi_2 = -0.3$, $\phi_3 = -0.7$, $\phi_4 = 0.1$, $\phi_5 = -0.9$, and $\phi_6 = -0.2$. The goal was to perform time series clustering with the Euclidean distance and (13). Hierarchical methods with complete linkage using both measures were implemented to evaluate whether the methods are capable of capturing the correlation structure between the sequences described above. We used the distance measure (13) under the tuning function (14) for $h = 1$, and $k = 3$. That is, the correlation structure contributes 90.5% to D, whereas the proximity with respect to values contributes 9.5%.

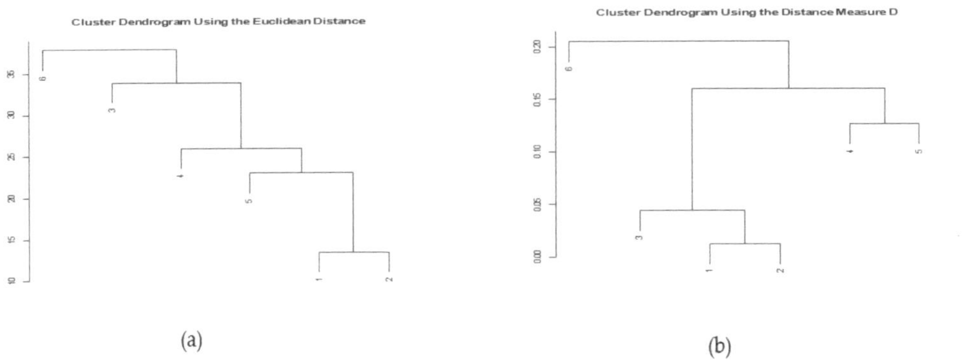

Figure 5. a) Time series clustering using the Euclidean distance, (b) Time series clustering using$D$.

In Figure 5, we see that the dendrogram obtained using hierarchical methods with the Euclidean distance does not recognize the correlation structure between $X^1$and X^3.In this case, sequences X^1, X^2, X^4, and $X^5$are pulled together before sequence X^3.However, hierarchical methods using (13) yield the expected results, combining sequences X^1, X^2, and X^3before the rest of the series.

To obtain better insight into the classification process using the proposed distance measure (13), we carried out a second simulation study that involves clustering measures based on other distances (but using the same setup). Observations from models 1-6 were generated using Gaussian white noise sequences for the errors, thereby preserving the same correlation structure used in the first study. The goal was to explore the ability of the distance measure (13) to group strongly correlated series first. A total of 1000 runs were considered for this

	d_E	d_{DTW}	d_M	d_F
Yes	65%	3%	99%	11%
No	35%	97%	1%	89%

Table 3. Percentage of correct clustering of the correlated series 1,2 and 3.

experiment, and 200 observations were generated in each run. We used measure (13) under the tuning function (14) for $h=1$, 2and $k=1$, 2, 3, 4.We counted the number of times that the hierarchical algorithm with complete linkage was able to pull together series 1, 2 and 3 before connecting them with other sequences. The traditional distances described in Section 2 were also implemented. After the 1000 simulation runs were finished, the percentage of times that the algorithm was able to recognize the correlated series was recorded. The results of the experiment are summarized in Table 3 and 4.

	$D_E(h,k)$	$D_{DTW}(h,k)$	$D_M(h,k)$	$D_F(h,k)$
	$h=1,k=1$	$h=1,k=1$	$h=1,k=1$	$h=1,k=1$
Yes	82%	60%	100%	13%
No	18%	40%	0	87%
	$h=1,k=2$	$h=1,k=2$	$h=1,k=2$	$h=1,k=2$
Yes	87%	68%	99%	22%
No	13%	32%	1%	78%
	$h=1,k=3$	$h=1,k=3$	$h=1,k=3$	$h=1,k=3$
Yes	90%	64%	99%	26%
No	10%	36%	1%	74%
	$h=1,k=4$	$h=1,k=4$	$h=1,k=4$	$h=1,k=4$
Yes	90%	65%	98%	29%
No	10%	35%	2%	71%
	$h=2,k=1$	$h=2,k=1$	$h=2,k=1$	$h=2,k=1$
Yes	83%	58%	100%	16%
No	17%	42%	0%	84%
	$h=2,k=2$	$h=2,k=2$	$h=2,k=2$	$h=2,k=2$
Yes	87%	59%	100%	26%
No	13%	41%	0%	74%
	$h=2,k=3$	$h=2,k=3$	$h=2,k=3$	$h=2,k=3$
Yes	90%	50%	100%	21%
No	10%	50%	0%	79%
	$h=2,k=4$	$h=2,k=4$	$h=2,k=4$	$h=2,k=4$
Yes	89%	56%	100%	26%
No	11%	44%	0%	74%

Table 4. Percentage of correct clustering of the correlated series (1,2, and 3). $D_{DTW}(h, k)$is distance measure (13) with the DTW distance. $D_M(h, k)$and $D_F(h, k)$denote distance measure (10) with Minkowski and Frechet distances respectively.

Note from Table 3 that the traditional distance measures failed to group the correlated sequences, with the exception of the Minkowski distance, which correctly grouped the correlated series 99% of the time. The hierarchical algorithm that uses the distance measure (13) has a higher percentage of well-clustered correlated sequences than the same algorithm using the traditional distance measures described in Section 2 (see Table 4). The percentage of correct clusters increased in all cases with the distance measure (13), suggesting that hierarchical algorithms can be improved by including coefficients of association that consider high-order cross-correlation.

3.5. The NDVI Data Set

In this section, we consider time series from four different locations in Argentina. The data set consists of 15 monthly NDVI series measured during a period of 19 years (i.e., January 1982-December 2000). The observed values correspond to a transformation to the interval

$[0, 255]$of the original NDVI series, which commonly resides in the interval $[-1, 1]$.The data were collected by a NOAA sensor at 1 km resolution and provided by the Comisión Nacional de Actividades Espaciales (CONAE) in Córdoba, Argentina. Fifteen time series were collected from the following: the Amazon region in the northeast of Argentina (1, 2, 3), the Patagonia region in the south of Argentina (4, 5, 6, 7), the Pampean region in the center of Argentina (8, 9, 10, 11) and the Pre-Andean zone of Argentina (12, 13, 14, 15). The time series are shown in Figure 6.

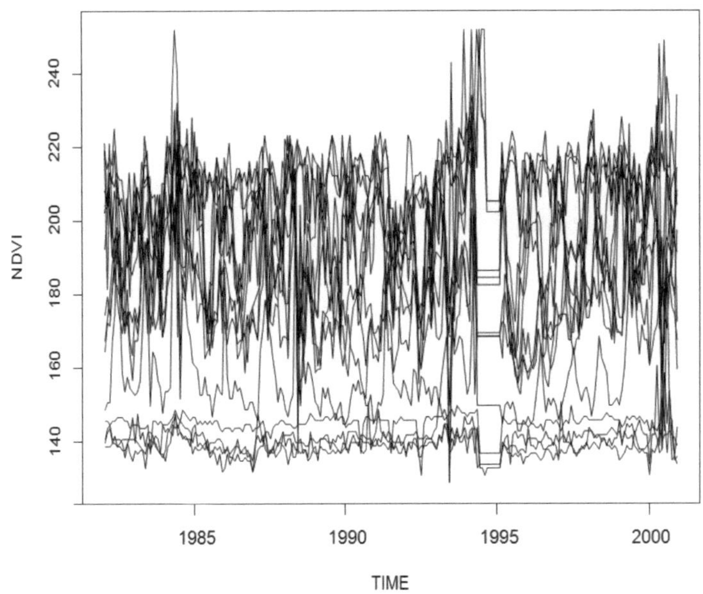

Figure 6. Fifteen NDVI series collected from four different regions in South America.

We can observe a variety of different patterns in Figure 6. In particular, the data collected during the period 1994-1995 show irregular behavior. Additionally, the original data lack some information (less than one percent) for all series over the period 1999-2000. An imputation technique based on moving averages, which takes into account past and future values of the series, was used to replace missing values. The series were grouped by geographical region and then plotted (Figure 7). Similar patterns are observed for the series across each group.

An exploratory data analysis was carried out for each of the 15 series. There exists significant autocorrelation of order of at least one in all series. Seasonal components are present in most of partial autocorrelations. Because there is no large departure from the weakly stationary assumptions (i.e., constant means and variances), all series can be modeled using the Box-Jenkins approach. Specifically, seasonal ARIMA models can be fitted to each single series with a small number of parameters (i.e., $p \leq 5$, $q \leq 5$and$d \leq 2$).

http://dx.doi.org/10.5772/50513

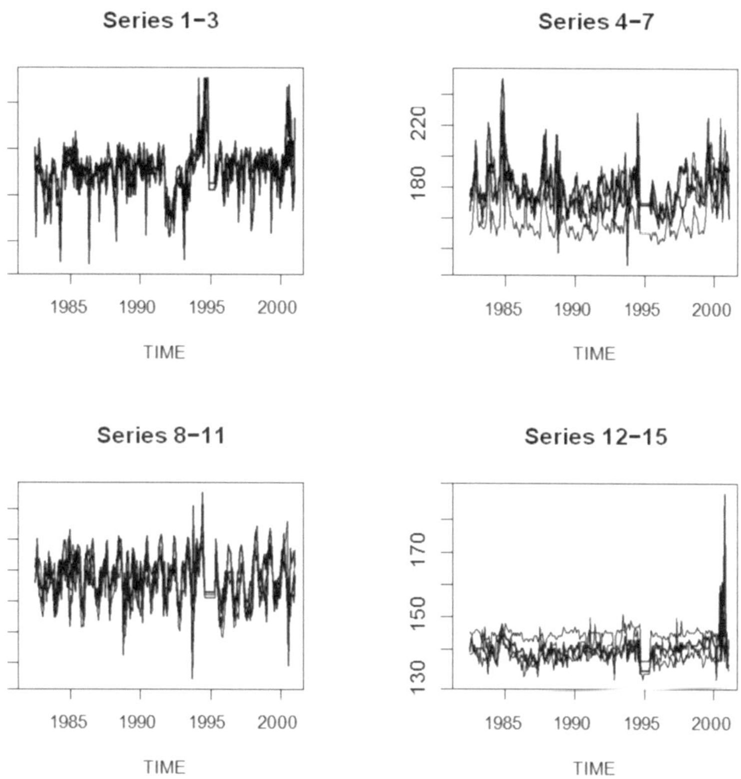

Figure 7. The fifteen NDVI series grouped by area.

3.6. Clustering

Using the NVDI data set described in Section 3.5, the distance measure Din (13) was computed for all possible pairs. Then, dendrogram plots were constructed using a hierarchical procedure (i.e., complete linkage) to compare the mergers and clusters produced using $D$with those produced using the conventional distances described in Section 2.2 and (13). In Figure 8, we observe the agglomeration produced by using the Euclidean distance (top left); the other five plots show the results produced by distance (13) for different values of $k$and h.The agglomeration algorithm using the Euclidean distance merges series 5 together with series 12-15 and thus does not preserve location when grouping series. However, with $k=1$and $h=1$ in (13), the location dependence of the 15 series is captured. Higher values of $k$and h do not modify the original clusters formed using$D$. In Figure 9, we see the clusters and merges yielded by using the Minkowski distance in (13). Note that series 4 is classified together with series 8, 9, 10 and 11 in the top left plot, but with $k=1$and $h=1$, the algorithm handles the series differently (shown in the top right plot) by merging together those series that are in the same location. The effects of higher values of $k$and h.are again negligible. The Fréchet distance produced unsatisfactory results. In this case, the hierarchical algorithm does not take into account the geographical location when using both the conventional distances measures and (13). For example, series 1, 2 and 3 were merged in different stages. Nevertheless, when $k$and h are increased, the algorithm using (13) still clusters the series by geographical location. Indeed, if our goal is to produce four clusters as before, the hierarchical algorithm with h =2and k=3 produces a geographically consistent agglomeration (dendrograms not shown here). The same analysis was performed using the hierarchical algorithm with the dynamic time warping distance measure. In this case, this distance measure produced an agglomeration by geographical location and thus did not need to be modified to capture serial correlation. The result yielded with (13) produced the same outcome for all values of $k$and h.

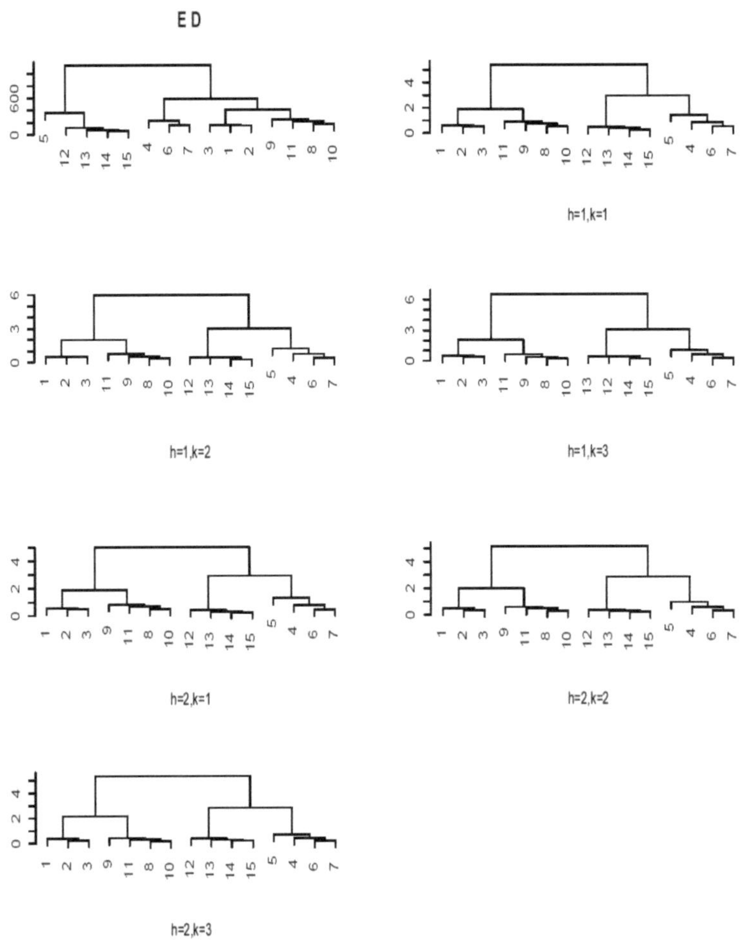

Figure 8. Clusters produced by using a hierarchical method with the Minkowski distance and (13).

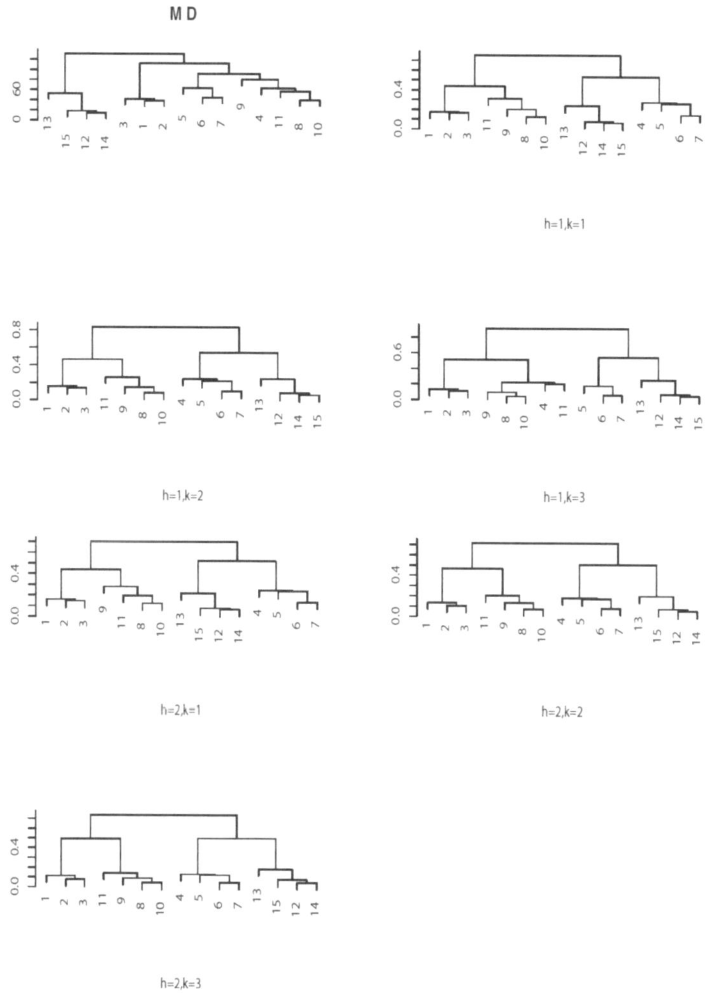

Figure 9. Clusters produced by using a hierarchical method with the Fréchet distance and (13)

4. Concluding Remarks and Future Work

This chapter described two problems. The first problem involved image segmentation, while the second problem involved clustering time series. For the first problem, a new algorithm was proposed that enhances the segmentation yielded by a previous algorithm (Ojeda et al., 2010). Identifying the best prediction window improves segmentation based on the estimation of AR-2D processes and generalizes the previous algorithm to different prediction windows associated with unilateral processes on the plane. An analysis of the association between the original and fitted images relies on the selection of a suitable image quality measure. Using three image quality coefficients that are commonly used in image segmentation, we carried out experiments that support our algorithm. Specifically, a set of images belonging to the image database (http://sipi.usc.edu/database/) were processed and provided satisfactory results (not shown here) in terms of image segmentation.

This chapter also proposed an extension of the dissimilarity measure first introduced in (Chouakria & Nagabhushan,2007). The simulation experiments performed and the data analysis carried out for relevant ecological series show that the distance lag h plays an important role in capturing the higher-order correlation of each series. Cluster analysis performed using the proposed distance measure produced different merges and dendrograms. Furthermore, the percentage of times that the hierarchical algorithms correctly classified the highly correlated sequences increased in all cases in which the distance measure (13) was used. For the NDVI series discussed in Section 3.5, the distance measure Dimproved the performance of the Euclidean, Fréchet and Minkowski distances in the presence of high-order autocorrelation in the series. The dynamic time warping distance measure showed the best performance in capturing the serial correlation between the NDVI series, and thus, it was not necessary to introduce modified distance measures such as (13) to ensure agglomeration by geographical location.

Now, further research for the topics presented in this chapter is outlined.

Following the notation used in the Algorithm 3, consider the following residual image.
$R_{W_i} = Z - \hat{Z}_{W_i}$.

One interesting open problem involves the characterization of the types of images and distributions associated with the segmentation produced by Algorithms 2 and 3. In addition, the definition and study of linear combinations of residual images produced by distinct prediction windows is also of interests. For example,

$$I = \sum_{j=1}^{4} a_j R_{W_i},$$

where $a_j$is a weight associated with the residual image R_{W_i}.

Regarding the clustering technique problem, the distribution of Dcan be studied from a parametric point of view. This is an open problem that we expect to address in future research.

Acknowledgements

The first author was partially supported by Fondecyt grant 1120048, UTFSM under grant 12.12.05, and Proyecto Basal CMM, Universidad de Chile. The second author was supported in part by CIEM-FAMAF, UNC, Argentina.

Author details

Ronny Vallejos[1*] and Silvia Ojeda[2]

*Address all correspondence to: ronny.vallejos@usm.cl

1 Department of Mathematics, Universidad Técnica Federico Santa María,, Chile

2 FAMAF, Universidad Nacional de Córdoba,, Argentina

References

[1] Allende, H., Galbiati, J., & Vallejos, R. (2001). Robust image modeling on image processing. *Pattern Recognition Letters*, 22(11), 1219 -1231.

[2] Baran, S., Pap, G. , & Zuijlen, M. C. A. (2004). Asymptotic inference for a nearly unstable sequence of stationary spatial AR models. *Statistics & Probability Letters*, 69(1), 53 -61.

[3] Basu, S., & Reinsel, G. (1993). Properties of the spatial unilateral first-order ARMA model. *Advances in Applied Probbability*, 25(3), 631 -648.

[4] Bustos, O., Ojeda, S., & Vallejos, R. (2009a). Spatial ARMA models and its applications to image filtering. *Brazilian Journal of Probability and Statistics*, 23(2), 141 -165 .

[5] Bustos, O., Ojeda, S., Ruiz, M., Vallejos, R., & Frery, A. (2009b). Asymptotic Behavior of RA-estimates in Autoregressive 2D Gaussian Processes. *Journal of Statistical Planning and Inference*, 139(10), 3649-3664.

[6] Cariou, C., & Chehdi, K. (2008). Unsupervised texture segmentation/classification usind 2-D autoregressive modeling and the stochastic expectation-maximization algorithm. *Pattern Recognition Letters*, 29(7), 905-917.

[7] Choi, B. (2000). On the asymptotic distribution of mean, autocovariance, autocorrelation, crosscovariance and impulse response estimators of a stationary multidimensional random field. *Communications in Statistics-Theory and Methods*, 29(8), 1703-1724.

[8] Chouakria, A. D., & Nagabhushan, P. N. (2007). Adaptive dissimilarity for measuring time series proximity. *Advances in Data Analysis and Classification*, 1(1), 5 -21 .

[9] Clifford, P., Richardson, S., & Hémon, D. (1989). Assessing the significance of the correlation between two spatial processes. *Biometrics*, 45(1), 123 -134.

[10] Cullis, B. R., & Glesson, A. C. (1991). Spatial analysis of field experiments-an extension to two dimensions. *Biometrics*, 47(4), 1449-1460.

[11] Francos, J., & Friedlander, B. (1998). Parameter estimation of two-dimensional moving average random fields. *IEEE Transaction Signal Processing*, 46(8), 2157-2165.

[12] Gaetan, C., & Guyon, X. (2010). *Spatial Statistics and Modelling*, Springer, New York.

[13] Genton, M. G., & Koul, H. L. (2008). Minimum distance inference in unilateral autoregressive laticce processes. *Statistica Sinica*, 18, 617-631.

[14] Golay, X., Kollias, S., Stoll, G., Meier, D., & Valavanis, A. (1998). A new correlation-based fuzzy logic clustering algorithm of FMRI. *Magnetic Resonance in Medicine*, 40(2), 249-260.

[15] Grondona, M. R., Crossa, J., Fox, P. N., & Pfeiffer, W. H. (1996). Analysis of variety yield trials using two-dimensional separable ARIMA processes. *Biometrics*, 52(2), 763-770.

[16] Guo, J., & Billard, L. (1998). Some inference results for causal autoregressive processes on a plane. *Journal of Time Series Analysis*, 19(6), 681-691.

[17] Guyon, X. (1982). Parameter estimation for a stationary process on a d-dimensional lattice. *Biometrika*, 69(1), 95-105.

[18] Ho, P. G. P. (2011). Image segmentation by autoregressive time series model. In Image Segmentation edited by Pei-Gee Ho. InTech.

[19] Illig, A., & Truong Van, B. (2006). Asymptotic results for spatial ARMA Models. *Communications in Statistics-Theory and Methods*, 35(4), 671 -688 .

[20] Jain, A. K., Murty, M. N., & Flynn, P. J. (1999). Data Clustering: A Review. *ACM Comput. Surveys,*, 31(3), 264-323.

[21] Kashyap, R., & Eom, K. (1988). Robust images techniques with an image restoration application. *IEEE Trans. Acoust. Speech Signal Process*, 36(8), 1313 -1325 .

[22] Mac, Queen. J. B. (1967). Some Methods for classification and Analysis of Multivariate Observations. *Proceedings of 5 -th Berkeley Symposium on Mathematical Statistics and Probability*, Berkeley, University of California Press, 1, 281-297.

[23] Martin, R. J. (1996). Some results on unilateral ARMA laticce processes. *Journal of Statistical Planning and Inference*, 50(3), 395-411.

[24] Matheron, G. (1965). Les Variables Régionalisées et leur Estimation Masson Paris.

[25] Politis, D. N., & Romano, J. P. (1994). The stationary bootstrap. *Journal of the American Statistical Association*, 89(428), 1303 -1313.

[26] Ojeda, S. M., Vallejos, R. O., & Lucini, M. (2002). Performance of RA Estimator for Bidimensional Autoregressive Models. *Journal of Statistical Simulation and Computation*, 72(1), 47 -62 .

[27] Ojeda, S. M., Vallejos, R., & Bustos, O. (2010). A New Image Segmentation Algorithm with Applications to Image Inpainting. .Computational Statistics & Data Analysis , 54(9), 2082 -2093 .

[28] Ojeda, S. M., Vallejos, R., & Lamberti, W. P. (2012). A Measure of Similarity Between Images. , in press Journal of Electronic Imaging.

[29] Quintana, C., Ojeda, S., Tirao, G., & Valente, M. (2011). Mammography image detection processing for automatic micro-calcification recognition. *Chilean Journal of Statistics*, 2(2), 69-79.

[30] Rukhin, A., & Vallejos, R. (2008). Codispersion coefficient for spatial and temporal series. *Statistics and Probability Letters*, 78(11), 1290 -1300 .

[31] Vallejos, R., & Mardesic, T. (2004). A recursive algorithm to restore images based on robust estimation of NSHP autoregressive models. *Journal of Computational and Graphical Statistics*, 13(3), 674 -682 .

[32] Vallejos, R., & Garcia-Donato, G. (2006). Bayesian analysis of contaminated quarter plane moving average models. *Journal of Statistical Computation and Simulation*, 76(2), 131-147.

[33] Vallejos, R. (2008). Assessing the association between two spatial or temporal sequences. *Journal of Applied Statistics*, 35(12), 1323 -1343 .

[34] Tjostheim, D. (1978). A measure of association for spatial variables. *Biometrika*, 65(1), 109 -114.

[35] Wang, Z., & Bovik, A. (2002). A universal image quality index. *IEEE Signal Processing Letters*, 9(3), 81 -84 .

Chapter 3

Image Segmentation Through an Iterative Algorithm of the Mean Shift

Roberto Rodríguez Morales, Didier Domínguez,
Esley Torres and Juan H. Sossa

Additional information is available at the end of the chapter

http://dx.doi.org/10.5772/50474

1. Introduction

Image analysis is a scientific discipline providing theoretical foundations and methods for solving problems appearing in a range of areas as diverse as biology, medicine, physics, astronomy, geography, chemistry, meteorology, robotics and industrial manufacturing, among others.

Inside any image analysis system, an aspect of vital importance for pattern recognition and image interpretation that has to be taken into account is segmentation and contour extraction. Both problems can be really difficult to face due to the variability in the form of the objects and the variation in the image quality. An example can be found in the case of biomedical images which are frequently affected by noise and sampling, that can cause considerable difficulties when rigid segmentation methods are applied [Chin-Hsing et al., 1998; Kenong & Levine, 1995; Koss et al., 1999; Rodríguez et al., 2002].

Many segmentation techniques are available in the literature and some of them have been widely used in different application problems. Most of these segmentation techniques were motivated by specific application purposes. Many different approaches for image segmentation there are; which mainly differ in the criterion used to measure the similarity of two regions and in the strategy applied to guide the segmentation process. The definition of suitable similarity and homogeneity measures is a fundamental task in many important applications, ranging from remote sensing to similarity-based retrieval in large image databases.

Segmentation is an important part of any computer vision and image analysis system, wherein regions of interest are identified and extracted for future processing. Of the quality of segmentation depends, on great measure, the good performance of higher level analysis steps such as recognition and interpretation.

However, in spite of the most complex algorithms developed until now, segmentation continues to be very application dependent. A single method that can solve the multitude of present problems there is not. It still remains a complex problem with no exact solution that by means of traditional low-level techniques, such as: thresholding, region growing and other classical operations requires a considerable amount of interactive guidance in order to attain satisfactory results. Automating these model-free approaches is difficult because of complexity, shadows, and variability within and across individual objects.

For years, the most suitable algorithms have been the iterative methods. These cover a variety of techniques, ranging from the mathematical morphology based methods, the deformable models up to thresholding based methods. However, one of the problems of these iterative techniques is the stopping criterion, for which many strategies have been proposed [Vincent & Soille, 1991; Cheriet et. al., 1998; Chenyang et. al., 2000].

Mean shift (MSH) is a robust technique which has been applied in many computer vision tasks, as by example: image segmentation, visual tracking, etc. [Shen & Brooks, 2007]. MSH technique was proposed by Fukunaga and Hostetler [Fukunaga et. al., 1975] and largely forgotten until Cheng´s paper [Cheng, 1995] rekindled interest in it. MSH is a versatile nonparametric density analysis tool and it can provide reliable solutions in many applications [Comaniciu, 2002]. In essence, MSH is an iterative mode detection algorithm in the density distribution space. The MSH procedure moves to a kernel-weighted average of the observations within a smoothing window. This computation is repeated until convergence is obtained at a *local* density mode. This way the density modes can be located without explicitly estimating the density. An elegant relation between the MSH and other techniques can be found in [Shen & Brooks, 2007].

The iterative algorithm that is used in this chapter is based on the mean shift and in several works was previously introduced and applied [Rodríguez & Suarez, 2006; Rodríguez, 2008; Domínguez & Rodríguez, 2009; Domínguez & Rodríguez, 2011; Rodríguez et. al., 2011a; Rodríguez et. al., 2011b; Rodríguez et. al., 2012]. In those papers, entropy was used as a stopping criterion. Entropy is not a new concept in the information theory field and it has been used in image restoration, edge detection and as an objective evaluation method for image segmentation [Zhang, 2003].

In this chapter is presented a research, using standard images and real images, based on a segmentation algorithm which used an iterative computation of the mean shift filtering. A comparison of the obtained results was carried out, according to the number of iterations and the degree of homogenization of the segmented images. Also, a comparison of the obtained results with our algorithm with other segmentation methods already established was carried out.

The aim of this chapter is to present the advances that the authors have obtained in the field of the image segmentation. Also, some strategies that constitute suitable tools are presented, which it can be used in many system of image analysis where methods of segmentation are required. The main contribution of this chapter is to analyze how the quality of the segmented images varies for different values of the window sizes (*hr* and *hs*) and the stopping criterion. Many of the obtained results were compared with other methods.

This chapter continues as follows: In Section 2 the most significant theoretical aspects on mean shift are detailed. In Section 3, we shortly introduce the entropy concept and we also give some comments on this. The iterative algorithm of the mean shift is described in Section 4. In Section 5 the used standard images are presented. Moreover, some of the characteristics of the real images are described. In Section 6 the experimental results are exposed, and also an analysis and discussion of these are carried out. Finally, in Section 7 the most important conclusions of this chapter are given.

2. Theoretical aspects

The iterative procedure to compute the mean shift is introduced as normalized density estimate of the gradient. By employing a differentiable kernel, an estimate of the density gradient can be defined as the gradient of the kernel density estimate; that is,

$$\hat{\nabla} f(x) = \nabla \hat{f}(x) = \frac{1}{nh^d} \sum_{i=1}^{n} \nabla K\left(\frac{x - x_i}{h}\right) \tag{1}$$

Conditions on the kernel $K(x)$ and the window radio h are derived in [Fukunaga & Hostetler, 1975] to guarantee asymptotic unbiasedness, mean-square consistency, and uniform consistency of the estimate in the expression (1). For a radial symmetry kernel,
$K(x) = C_k(\| x \|^2)$

where the profile is $r = \| x \|^2$, then; for example, for *Epanechikov* kernel (other choices are possible as will be seen below),

$$K_E(x) = \begin{cases} 1/2C_d^{-1}(d+2)(1 - \| x \|^2) \, if \, \| x \|^2 \leq 1 \\ 0 \qquad \qquad \qquad otherwise \end{cases}$$

The density gradient estimate becomes,

$$\hat{\nabla} f_E(x) = \frac{1}{n(h^d c_d)} \cdot \frac{d+2}{h^2} \sum_{x_i \in S_h(x)} (x_i - x) = \frac{n_x}{n(h^d c_d)} \cdot \frac{d+2}{h^2} \left(\frac{1}{n_x} \sum_{x_i \in S_h(x)} (x_i - x) \right) \tag{2}$$

where the region $S_h(x)$ is a hypersphere of radius h having volume $h^d c_d$, centered at x, and containing n_x data points; that is, the uniform kernel. The last term in expression (2) is called the *sample mean shift*,

$$M_{h,U}(x) = \frac{1}{n_x} \sum_{x_i \in S_h(x)} (x_i - x) = \frac{1}{n_x} \sum_{x_i \in S_h(x)} x_i - x \tag{3}$$

The quantity $\frac{n_x}{n\,(h^d c_d)}$ is the kernel density estimate $\hat{f}_U(x)$ (the uniform *kernel*) computed with the hypersphere$S_h(x)$, and thus we can write the expression (2) as:

$$\hat{\nabla} f_E(x) = \hat{f}_U(x) \cdot \frac{d+2}{h^2} M_{h,U}(x) \tag{4}$$

which yields,

$$M_{h,U}(x) = \frac{h^2}{d+2} \frac{\hat{\nabla} f_E(x)}{\hat{f}_U(x)} \tag{5}$$

Expression (5) shows that an estimate of the normalized gradient can be obtained by computing the sample mean shift in a uniform kernel centered on x. In addition, the mean shift has the direction of the gradient of the density estimate at x when this estimate is obtained with the *Epanechnikov* kernel. Since the mean shift vector always points towards the direction of the maximum increase in the density, it can define a path leading to a local density maximum; that is, to a mode of the density (see Fig. 1).

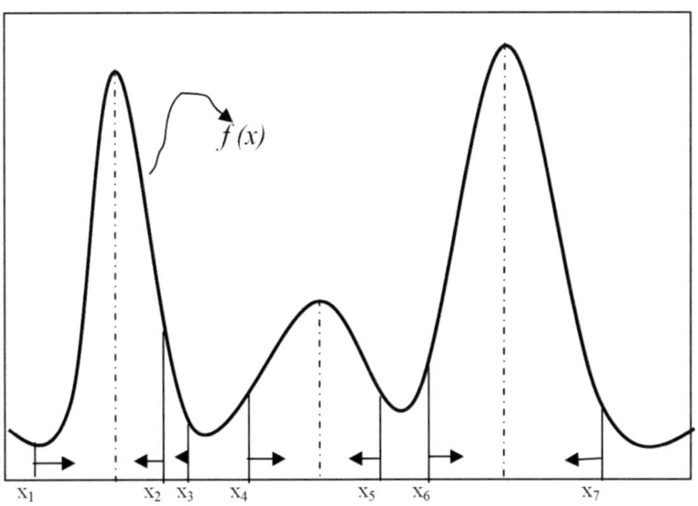

Figure 1. Gradient mode clustering.

In addition, expression (5) shows that the mean is shifted towards the region in which the majority of the points reside. Since the mean shift is proportional to the local gradient estimate, it can define a path leading to a stationary point of the estimated density, where these stationary points are the modes. Moreover, as it was pointed out the normalized gradient in expression (5) introduces a desirable adaptive behavior, since the mean shift step is large for low density regions corresponding to valleys, and decreases as x approaches a mode. This is possible to see in a clear way in Figure 2.

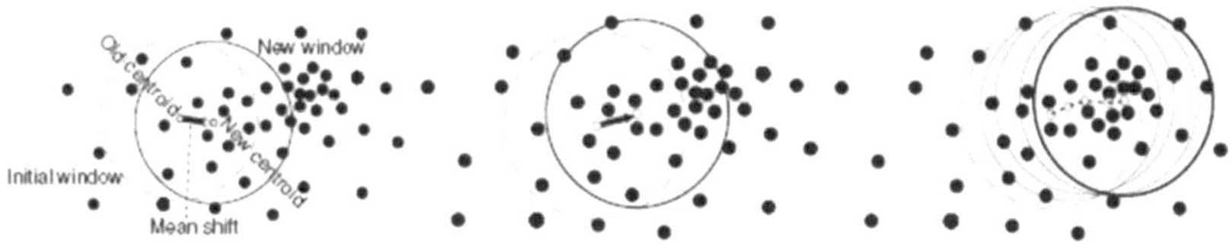

Figure 2. Local maxima of the probability density given by samples.

Mathematically speaking, this is justified since $\frac{\hat{\nabla} f_E(x)}{\hat{f}_U(x)} > \hat{\nabla} f_E(x)$. Thus the corresponding step size for the same gradient will be greater than that nearer mode. This will allow observations far from the mode or near a local minimum to move towards the mode faster than using $\hat{\nabla} f_E(x)$ alone.

In [Comaniciu & Meer, 2002] it was proven that the *mean shift procedure*, obtained by successive:

- computing the mean shift vector $M_h(x)$
- translating the window $S_h(x)$ by $M_h(x)$,

guarantees convergence.

Therefore, if the individual mean shift procedure is guaranteed to converge, it is hoped that a recursively procedure of the mean shift also converges. In other words, if we consider an iterative procedure like the individual sum of many procedures of the mean shift and each individual procedure converges; then, the iterative procedure also converges. The question that continues open is when to stop the recursive procedure. The answer is in the use of the entropy, as it will be shown in next Section.

2.1. Generalization

Employing the profile notation the density estimate can be written as [Comaniciu, 2000],

$$\hat{f}_K(x) = \frac{1}{nh^d} \sum_{i=1}^{n} k\left(\left\| \frac{x-x_i}{h} \right\|^2 \right) \quad (6)$$

By denoting with $g = -k'$, that is, the profile defined by the derivative of profile k with the sign changed (we assume that the derivative of k exits $\forall\, x \in [0, \infty)$), excepting a finite set of points), then the density gradient estimate (see expression (1)) becomes,

$$\hat{\nabla} f_K(x) = \nabla \hat{f}_K(x) = \frac{2}{nh^{d+2}} \sum_{i=1}^{n} (x - x_i) k'\left(\left\| \frac{x - x_i}{h} \right\|^2\right)$$
$$= \frac{2}{nh^{d+2}} \left[\sum_{i=1}^{n} g\left(\left\| \frac{x - x_i}{h} \right\|^2\right) \right] \left[\frac{\sum_{i=1}^{n} x_i g\left(\left\| \frac{x - x_i}{h} \right\|^2\right)}{\sum_{i=1}^{n} g\left(\left\| \frac{x - x_i}{h} \right\|^2\right)} - x \right] \tag{7}$$

where $\sum_{i=1}^{n} g\left(\left\| \frac{x - x_i}{h} \right\|^2\right)$ is assumed to be nonzero.

One can observe that the derivate of the *Epanechnikov* profile is the uniform profile, while the derivate of the normal profile remains as exponential.

The last bracket in expression (7) contains the mean shift vector computed with a kernel *G(x)* defined by $G(x) = cg(\| x \|^2)$, where c is a normalization constant, that is,

$$M_{h,G}(x) = \frac{\sum_{i=1}^{n} x_i g\left(\left\| \frac{x - x_i}{h} \right\|^2\right)}{\sum_{i=1}^{n} g\left(\left\| \frac{x - x_i}{h} \right\|^2\right)} - x = \frac{\sum_{i=1}^{n} x_i G\left(\frac{x - x_i}{h}\right)}{\sum_{i=1}^{n} G\left(\frac{x - x_i}{h}\right)} - x \tag{8}$$

Then, the density estimate at x becomes,

$$\hat{f}_G(x) = \frac{1}{nh^d} \sum_{i=1}^{n} G\left(\frac{x - x_i}{h}\right) = \frac{c}{nh^d} \sum_{i=1}^{n} g\left(\left\| \frac{x - x_i}{h} \right\|^2\right) \tag{9}$$

By using the expressions (8) y (9), the expression (7) becomes,

$$\hat{\nabla} f_K(x) = \hat{f}_G(x) \cdot \frac{2}{h^2 c} M_{h,G}(x) \tag{10}$$

from where it follows that,

$$M_{h,G}(x) = \frac{h^2 c}{2} \frac{\hat{\nabla} f_K(x)}{\hat{f}_G(x)} \tag{11}$$

Expression (11) is a generalization of the mean shift vector. This allows to use other kernels; for example, Gauss kernel, which gives wonderful results.

On the other hand, a digital image can be represented as a two-dimensional array of p-dimensional vectors (pixels), where $p=1$ in the gray level case, three for color images, and $p>3$ in the multispectral case. As was pointed in [Comaniciu & Meer, 2002] when the location and range vectors are concatenated in the joint spatial-range domain of dimension $d=p+2$, their different nature has to be compensated by proper normalization of parameters h_s and h_r. Thus, the multi-variable kernel is defined as the product of two radially symmetric kernels and the Euclidean metric allows a single bandwidth for each domain, that is:

$$K_{h_s,h_r}(x)=\frac{C}{h_s^2\,h_r^p}\,k\left(\left\|\frac{x^s}{h_s}\right\|^2\right)k\left(\left\|\frac{x^r}{h_r}\right\|^2\right) \tag{12}$$

where x^s is the spatial part, x^r is the range part of a feature vector, $k(x)$ the common profile used in both domains, h_s and h_r the employed kernel bandwidths, and C the corresponding normalization constant.

One can observe in Figure 2 that the $l_2$norm is implicitly used in order to define the neighborhoods of pixels. From a mathematical point of view the concept of norm is associated with the size of the elements of a given space. Given a linear space L over a field K and an element $x\in L$ is defined as norm of x, denoted$\|x\|$, a finite functional which satisfies some conditions [Domínguez & Rodríguez, 2009]. As we have pointed out, when $S_h(x)$is defined as expression (2) implicitly makes use of the l_2 norm defined as,$\|x\|_2=\sqrt{\sum_{j=1}^{d}x_j^2}$, $x\in\Re^d$, since $S_h(x)=\{x':\|x-x'\|_2\le h\}$.

Note that in order to verify the condition $x_i\in S_h(x)$ in (2), for each $x_i$it is necessary to calculate $\|x-x_i\|_2$which entails conducting d elevations to the second power, d-1 sums and calculating one square root. Verifying the same condition using the l_∞ norm, defined as $\|x\|_\infty=\max_j|x_j|$ only involves calculating the maximum value in the module of components of the difference vector$x-x_i$.

In [Domínguez & Rodríguez, 2009; Domínguez & Rodríguez, 2011], we carried out a theoretical and practical study related with this issue. We proved the convergence of the mean shift by using the l_∞ norm. The convergence of mean shift for discrete data was proved in [Comaniciu, 2000] using the l_2 norm for defining the hypersphere$S_h(x)$. The following theorem guarantees the convergence when it replaces the l_2 norm by the l_∞norm. The proof is similar to the theorem proved in [Comaniciu, 2000] and it can be found in [Domínguez & Rodríguez, 2011].

Theorem 1

Let $\hat{f}_E = \left\{ \hat{f}_k (y_k, K_E) \right\}$ *the sequence of density estimates obtained using Epanechnikov kernel and computed in the points* y_k *defined by the successive locations of the mean shift procedure with uniform kernel and N(x), denoting* $\| x \|_N$, *a norm that satisfies* $N(x) \leq \| x \|_2, \ \forall x \in \Re^d$. *If the hypersphere* $S_h(y_k)$ *is defined using N(x)* $\forall k \in И$, *then the sequence is convergent.*

As a direct consequence of this theorem, the mean shift algorithm converge using the l_∞ norm when defining the hypersphere $S_h(x)$because $\| x \|_\infty \leq \| x \|_2, \ \forall x \in \Re^d$.

3. Entropy

From the point of view of digital image processing, entropy of an image *I* is defined as:

$$E(I) = -\sum_{x=0}^{2^B-1} p(x) log_2 p(x) \qquad (13)$$

where *B* is the total quantity of bits of the digitized image and by agreement $log_2(0)=0$; $p(x)$ is the probability of occurrence of a gray-level value. Within a totally uniform region, entropy reaches the minimum value. Theoretically speaking, the probability of occurrence of the gray-level value, within a uniform region is always one. In practice, when one works with real images the entropy value does not reach, in general, the zero value. This is due to the existent noise in the image. Therefore, if we consider entropy as a measure of the disorder within a system, it can be used as a good stopping criterion, by the use of the mean shift filtering, for an iterative process. Entropy within each region diminishes in measure in that the regions become more homogeneous, and at the same time in the whole image, until reaching a stable value. When convergence is reached, a totally segmented image is obtained, because the mean shift filtering is not idempotent. In addition, as in [Comaniciu & Meer, 2002] was pointed out, the mean shift based image segmentation procedure is a straightforward extension of the discontinuity preserving smoothing algorithm and the segmentation step does not add a significant overhead to the filtering process.

The choice of entropy as a measure of goodness deserves several observations. Entropy reduction diminishes the randomness in corrupted probability density function and tries to counteract noise. Then, by following this analysis, as the segmented image is a simplified version of the original image, entropy of the segmented image should be smaller. Recently, it was empirically found that the entropy of the noise diminishes faster than that of the signal [Suyash et. al., 2006]. Therefore, an effective criterion to stop would be when the relative rate of change of the entropy from one iteration to the next, falls below a given threshold. All these observations were the main motivation in seeking a segmentation procedure from the iterations of the mean shift filtering. This new algorithm is much simpler [Rodríguez & Suarez, 2006].

http://dx.doi.org/10.5772/50474

4. Algorithms

In general, an image captured with a real physical device is contaminated with noise and in most cases a statistical model of white noise is assumed, mean zero and variance σ. For smoothing or elimination of this form of noise many types of filters have been published, the most classic being the low pass filter. This filter indiscriminately replaces the central pixel in a window by the average or the weighted average of pixels contained therein. The end result with this filtering is a blurred image; since this reduces the noise but also important information is taken away from the edges. However, there are low pass filtering techniques that preserve the discontinuities and reduce abrupt changes near local structures. A diverse number of approaches have been published taking into consideration the use of adaptive filtering. These range from an adaptive Wiener filter, local isotropic smoothing, to an anisotropic filtering. The mean shift works in the spatial-range domain, but differs from it in the use of local information. The algorithm that was proposed in [Comaniciu & Meer, 2002] for filtering through mean shift is as follows:

Let $\{x_i\}_i$ and$\{z_i\}_i$, $i=1, \ldots, n$ be the input and filtered images in the joint spatial-range domain. For each pixel$p \in x_i$, $p=(x, y, z) \in \Re^3$, where $(x, y) \in \Re^2$ and$z \in [0, 2^{\beta}-1]$, β being the quantity of bits/pixel in the image. The filtering algorithm comprises the following steps:

For each $i=1, \ldots, n$

1. Initialize $j=1$ and $y_{i,1} = p_i$.
2. Compute the mean shift in order to obtain the mode where the pixel converges; that is, the calculation of the mean shift is carried out until convergence, $y = y_{i,c}$.
3. Store at Z_i the component of the gray level of calculated value:$Z_i = (x_i^s, y_{i,c}^r)$, where x_i^s is the spatial component and $y_{i,c}^r$ is the range component.

4.1. Segmentation algorithm by recursively applying the mean shift filtering

4.1.1. Algorithm No. 1

Let *ent1* be the initial value of the entropy of the first iteration. Let *ent2* be the second value of the entropy after the first iteration. Let *errabs* be the absolute value of the difference of entropy between the first and the second iteration. Let *edsEnt* be the threshold to stop the iterations; that is, to stop when the relative rate of change of the entropy from one iteration to the next, falls below this threshold. Then, the segmentation algorithm comprises the following steps:

1. Initialize *ent2 = 1, errabs = 1, edsEnt = 0.001.*
2. While *errabs* > *edsEnt,* then
3. Filter the image according to the steps of the previous algorithm; store in $Z^{[k]}$ the filtered image.
4. Calculate the entropy from the filtered image according to expression (8); store in *ent1*.

5. Calculate the absolute difference with the entropy value obtained in the previous step; *errabs = /ent1 – ent2/*

6. Update the value of the parameter; *ent2 = ent1*; $Z^{[k+1]} = Z^{[k]}$

It can be observed that, in this case, the proposed segmentation algorithm is a direct extension of the filtering algorithm, which ends when the entropy reaches stability. The effectiveness of this algorithm will be proven along this chapter. In this work the thresholding value (*edsEnt*) was empirically obtained. Recent investigations have proven that smaller values of the threshold do not affect, qualitatively nor quantitatively in dependence on original image, the final result of the segmentation. One will be able to see these results in this chapter. More details and discussion on this issue will be given in the next section.

In [Christoudias et. al., 2002], it was stated that the recursive application of the mean shift property yields a simple mode detection procedure. The modes are the local maxima of the density. Therefore, with the new segmentation algorithm, by recursively applying mean shift, convergence is guaranteed. Indeed, the proposed algorithm is a straightforward extension of the filtering process. In [Comanociu, 2000], it was proven that the mean shift procedure converges. In other words, one can consider the new segmentation algorithm as a concatenated application of individual mean shift filtering operations. Therefore, if we consider the whole event as linear, the recursive algorithm converges.

4.1.2. Algorithm No. 2: Binarization algorithm by recursively applying the mean shift filtering

This algorithm is very similar to the algorithm *No. 1*, only that in this occasion two steps are added. This continue of this way,

1. Initialize *ent2 = 1, errabs = 1, edsEnt = 0.001.*

2. While *errabs > edsEnt*, then

   - 2.1. Filter the image according to the steps of the previous algorithm; store in Z [*k*] the filtered image.

   - 2.2. Calculate the entropy from the filtered image according to expression (6); store in *ent1*.

   - 2.3. Calculate the absolute difference with the entropy value obtained in the previous step; *errabs = /ent1– ent2/.*

   - 2.4. Update the value of the parameter; *ent2 = ent1*; *Z[k +1] = Z[k].*

3. To carry out a parametric logarithm (*parlog = 70, this is the parameter*).

4. Binarization: to assign to the background the white color and to the objects the black color.

In the experimentation was proven that the final result is not very sensitive to this parameter, because a variation in the range from 60 to 90 led to the same result [Rodriguez, 2008].

5. Used standard images and utilized real images. Some characteristics

In Figure 3 a representation of the used standard images for this research appear. Some characteristics on these standard images can be commented.

Figure 3. Standard images. (a) Cosmonaut, (b) Baboon, (c) Barbara, (d) Bird, (e) Cameraman, (f) Peppers, (g) Lake, (h) Mountain, (i) Lena.

For example, one can observe that some of these images are rich in high frequencies (Baboon and Barbara), other are rich in low frequencies (Bird and Peppers, these have more homogeneous zones) while other images have both, low and high frequencies (Cosmonaut and Cameraman). These characteristics will influence on the behavior of iterative algorithm, in particular, on the number of iterations. This issue will be deeply analyzed in Section of experimental results.

Other real images used in this work can be seen in Figure 4. These images are biopsies, which represent an angiogenesis process in malignant tumors. These were included in paraffin by using the inmunohistoquimic technique with the complex method of avidina biotina. Finally, monoclonal CD34 was contrasted with green methyl to accentuate formation of new blood vessels (angiogenesis process). These biopsies were obtained from soft parts of human bodies and the images were captured via MADIP system with a resolution of 512x512x8 bit/pixels [Rodríguez et. al., 2001].

Several notable characteristics of these images there are; which are common to typical images that we encounter in the tissues of biopsies. For example, the intensity is slightly darker within the blood vessel than in the local surrounding background. It is emphasized that this observation holds only within the local surroundings. In addition, due to acquisition protocol, the images are corrupted with a lot of noise. For more details on these images refer to [Rodríguez et. al., 2005].

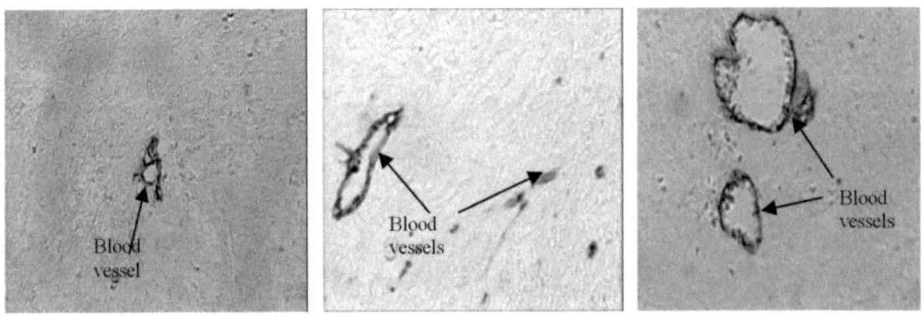

Figure 4. These images represent the angiogenesis process. The blood vessels are marked with arrows.

6. Experimental results and discussion

Image segmentation, that is, classification of the image intensity-level values into homogeneous areas is recognized to be one of the most important steps in any image analysis system. Homogeneity, in general, is defined as similarity among the pixel values, where a piecewise constant model is enforced over the image [Comaniciu and Meer, 2002].

All the segmentation experiments in this work were performed by using a uniform kernel. In order to be effective the comparison of the obtained results with our algorithm and with the *EDISON* system [Christoudias et. al., 2002], the same parameters (*hr* and *hs*), in both procedures, were used.

The value of *hs* is related to the spatial resolution of the analysis while the value *hr* defines the range resolution. It is necessary to note that the spatial resolution *hs* has a different effect on the output image when compared to the gray level resolution (*hr, spatial range*). Only features with large spatial support are represented in the segmented image with our algorithm when *hs* is increased. On the other hand, only features with high contrast survive when *hr* is large. Therefore, the quality of segmentation is controlled by the spatial value *hs* and the range (gray level) *hr*, resolution parameters defining the radii of the (3D/2D) windows in the respective domains. As our algorithm is a direct extension of the filtering algorithm similar behavior was also reported in [Comaniciu and Meer, 2002]. In addition, as our algorithm does not need parameter *M*, for the effects of the comparison the same one was set to $M = 1$ in the *EDISON* system.

The first preliminary results when applying our algorithm were published in the year 2006 [Rodríguez & Suarez, 2006]. In those researchers a quantitative comparison was not carried out, the comparison was only visual. The aim of that moment was alone to give to know the existence of our algorithm and to carry out a comparison with another established already [Christoudias et. al., 2002]. A deeper explanation on the characteristics of our algorithm was published in the year 2011[Rodríguez et. al., 2011a]. Nevertheless, two examples of the results reached in the year 2006 appear in the Figure 5 and 6.

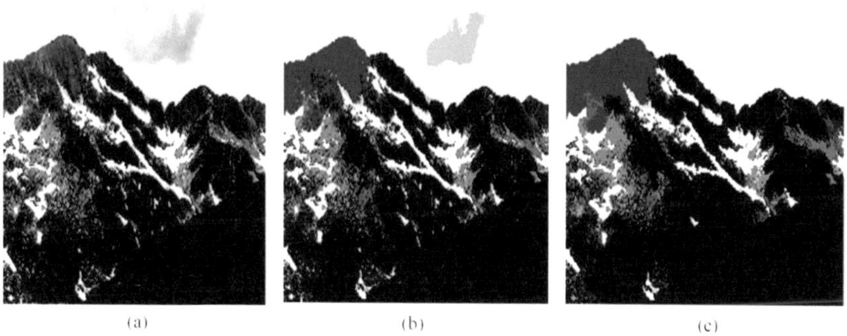

Figure 5. a) Original image, (b) Segmented image according to our algorithm *(hs, hr) = (12, 15)*, (c) Segmented image by using *EDISON* system *(hs, hr, M) = (12, 15, 1)*.

Figure 6. a) Original image, (b) Segmented image by our strategy *(hs, hr)* = (*12, 15*), (c) Segmented image according to *EDISON* system, (*hs, hr, M*) = (*12, 15, 1*). The arrows in the Fig. 2(b) indicate better segmented regions.

From the point of view of the final result, the image segmented with our algorithm has a more natural aspect. In many occasions, given the application, segmentation imposes certain conditions (elimination of regions, pruning or integration of certain maxima, etc). This can originate a biased image with regard to the original image. With our algorithm the resolution is only imposed on the segmentation process; that is, the parameters *hr* and *hs*. For this reason, our algorithm does not make mistakes; that is, a segmented image, very different to the original image, is not obtained. This is one of the most important experimental results obtained with our algorithm.

It is important to point out that with both algorithms (the proposed one and the *EDISON* system) very similar results were obtained (only differences in very few regions; see the arrows). The substantial difference between both algorithms is the one shown in Fig. 6(c), it was necessary to carry out a filtering step and later on a segmentation step. In this last step, one can have certain complexity when adjacency graphs and hierarchical techniques are used [Comaniciu, 2000]. With our algorithm the segmented image is directly obtained from the filtering process. However, it is necessary to have in mind that segmentation is very dependent on the application. For this reason, in order to compare our proposal with *EDISON* system, the most remarkable differences were looked for.

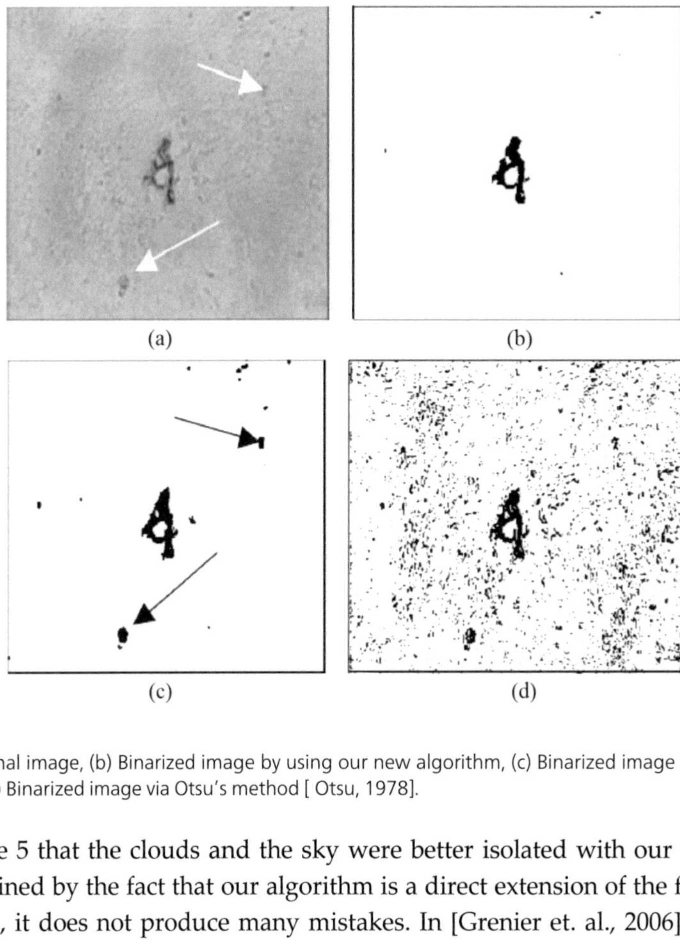

Figure 7. a) Original image, (b) Binarized image by using our new algorithm, (c) Binarized image by using graph [Rodriguez, 2008], (d) Binarized image via Otsu's method [Otsu, 1978].

Note in Figure 5 that the clouds and the sky were better isolated with our algorithm. This result is explained by the fact that our algorithm is a direct extension of the filtering process and, therefore, it does not produce many mistakes. In [Grenier et. al., 2006] the mean shift filtering was also iteratively applied in order to increase the smoothing effect. However, the difference with our algorithm is that in that work a stopping criterion was not given. The authors iterated the mean shift 10 times before starting the segmentation process.

A direct application of our algorithm for the binarization of blood vessels in an angiogenesis process was published in [Rodriguez, 2008]. Two examples appear in the Figures 7 and 8. In the year 2005 were obtained a similar result with a more complicated algorithm [Rodríguez et. al., 2005].

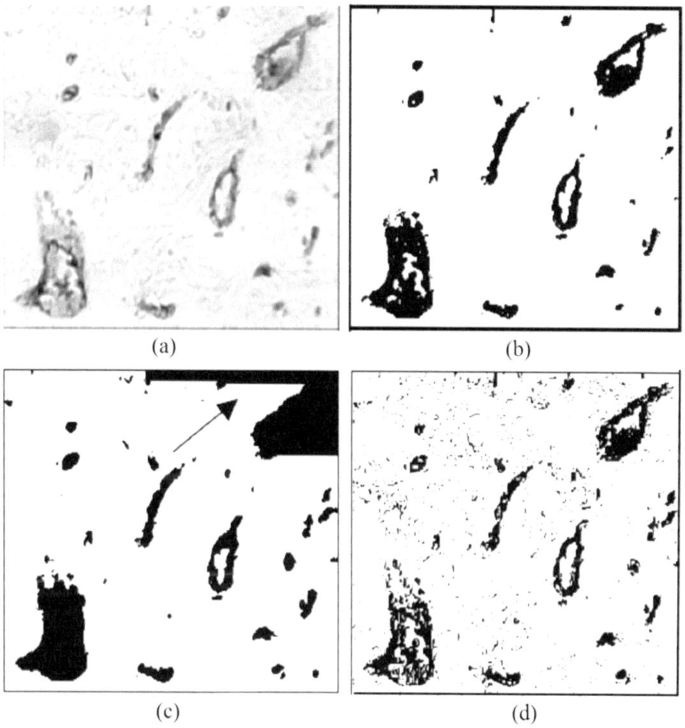

Figure 8. a) Original image, (b) Binarized image by using our new algorithm, (c) Binarized image by using graph, (d) Binarized image via Otsu's method.

It is evident to observe that the binarized image by using the new algorithm has a better appearance than the obtained image by using graph. Note, in this case, that the binarization algorithm by using graph made a mistake (see arrow in Figure 8 (c)). In practice, it has been proven that this behavior did not always happen with all images and in the corners of the images this was manifested fundamentally. We note in Figures 7 and 8 that the binarized image using the algorithm No. 2 was cleaner and it did not accentuate the spurious information that appears in the original image (see arrows in Figure 7(a)). According to criterion of pathologists these objects (spurious, with little contrast) were originated by a problem in the preparation of the samples. The obtained result by using Otsu's method is evident, a lot of noisy arose. This best result with the new binarization algorithm is because the same one is a direct extension of the filtering process. The parameter used to carry out the parametric logarithm was similar to 70 and this value was the same for all the binarized images. For more details on these results see [Rodriguez, 2008].

As it was expressed previously the $l_2$norm is implicitly used in order to define the neighborhoods of pixels when working with the mean shift. An interesting issue is to analyze that it happens when substituting the $l_2$norm by the l_∞ norm. In such a sense, we will show a series of experiments conducted with the aim of comparing, in terms of execution time and degree of homogenization, the obtained results by two segmentation algorithms. The graphic of the time spent by both algorithms on a group of standard images is presented and analyzed. In order to carry out the comparison of the obtained results the same parameters ($h_r = 15$ and $h_s = 4$) in both procedures, by using the l_∞norm and the l_2 norm were used.

In Fig. 9 (c), the segmentation of the image *Astro* is presented by using the algorithm *No.1* described in *Section 2.3.1*. In Fig. 9 (b) the result using the algorithm that makes use of the l_∞ norm is shown. In Fig. 9 (b) it can be seen that the segmented image using the l_∞norm presents a greater degree of homogenization. Comparing these images visually, it is evident that the use of the l_∞ norm leads to a greater similarity in the value of intensity of certain groupings of pixels (see Earth zone). This greater degree of homogenization can be seen as an advantage if the algorithm is used in an application where one wants to extract the figure of the astronaut. However, in an application where the objects of interest are the clouds, their elimination would become a drawback. This corroborates that the segmentation is heavily dependent on the application.

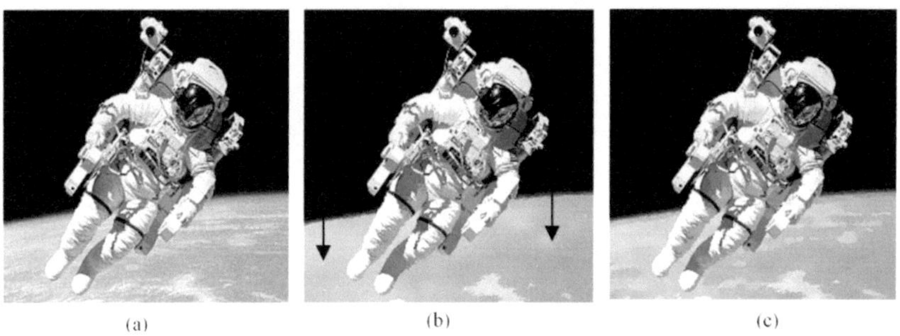

Figure 9. a) Original image, (b) Segmented image using the l_∞norm, (c) Segmented image using the $l_2$norm.

Figure 10. a) Original image, (b) Segmented image using the l_∞ norm, (c) Segmented image using the l_2 norm.

Other example of segmentation is presented in Figure 10 by using standard images. As in the previous example, there is again a greater homogenization when the neighborhood by using the l_∞ norm is defined. In this case, from a standpoint of a visual comparison, in Figure 10(b) the arrows indicate parts of major homogenization. For example, in the image of Figure 10(c), where the $l_2$norm is used, the boxes indicate parts which have a lesser degree of homogeneity between the pixels that represent the grass of the field.

Figure 11 shows a graphic of the execution times of the algorithms that make use of the l_∞ and l_2 norms. The values of the runtime for each image using the $l_2$norm in the definition of $S_h(x)$are represented by circles, while the squares represent the runtime associated with the l_∞norm. As is shown in Figure 11, in general, the runtime of the algorithm that makes use of the l_∞norm is higher than using the l_2 norm.

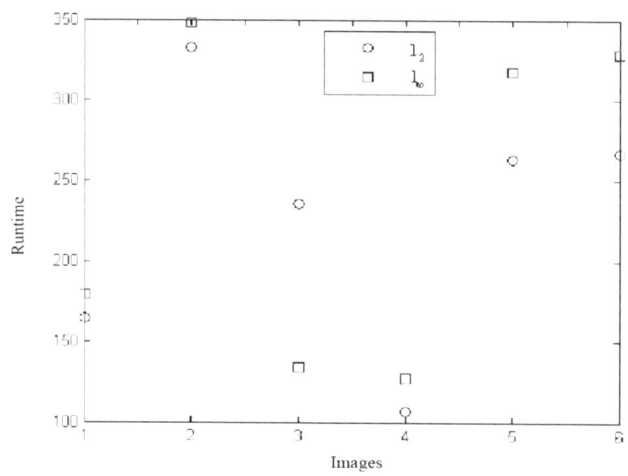

Figure 11. Runtime of the algorithms for standard images.

The greater homogenization observed using the l_∞norm to define$S_h(x)$ suggests the search for values h_s and hr in order to obtain more efficient results and smaller runtime. The readers interested in deepening in these results to see [Domínguez & Rodríguez, 2009].

Another issue that attracted the attention of the authors was the theoretical demonstration of the mean shift when the l_∞norm is used. The convergence of the algorithm by using the l_∞ norm was empirically shown through an extensive experimentation [Domínguez & Rodríguez, 2009]. In [Domínguez & Rodríguez, 2011] was proven a theorem which guarantees the convergence of the l_∞norm instead of the l_2 norm in order to define the region$S_h(x)$. The convergence of mean shift for discrete data was proved in [Comaniciu, 2000] using the l_2 norm for defining the hypersphere$S_h(x)$.

Table 1 shows the obtained results using *hr=8* and *hs=2*. As can be seen, for these values, execution times were lower using the$l_2$norm. The values were comparable with those obtained using the l_∞ norm in order to define the neighborhoods of the pixels and the maximum difference between the runtimes was 96,876 seconds, which was obtained with the image Baboon.

Image	Norm	hr	hs	Time
Cosmonaut256	l_2	8	2	186.1410
Cosmonaut256	l_∞	8	2	207.6880
Baboon256	l_2	8	2	76.4370
Baboon256	l_∞	8	2	173.3130
Barbara256	l_2	8	2	96.6570
Barbara256	l_∞	8	2	156
Bird256	l_2	8	2	82.7810
Bird256	l_∞	8	2	78.6250
Cameraman256	l_2	8	2	124.0470
Cameraman256	l_∞	8	2	209.2030
Peppers256	l_2	8	2	94.0780

Table 1.

Image	Norm	hr	hs	Time
Cosmonaut 256	l_2	15	4	164.8590
Cosmonaut 256	l_∞	15	4	179.2660
Baboon256	l_2	15	4	332.5160
Baboon256	l_∞	15	4	348.3130
Barbara256	l_2	15	4	235.2970
Barbara256	l_∞	15	4	134.0780
Bird256	l_2	15	4	107.2810
Bird256	l_∞	15	4	127.0630
Cameraman256	l_2	15	4	263.4380
Cameraman256	l_∞	15	4	317.1870
Peppers256	l_2	15	4	267.2650
Peppers256	l_∞	15	4	328.3590

Table 2.

In Table 2, it can be seen that for window sizes $hr=15$ and $hs=4$ the runtime was in favour of the $l_2$norm (difference of 61,094 seconds). This result was obtained with the image Peppers.

However, one can observe that in most of the images the difference of the runtimes were decreased when the values *hr=8* and *hs=2* were used (see Table 1). Moreover, in case of image Barbara the runtime using the l_∞ norm was smaller than the runtime using $l_2$norm. The difference was 101.219 seconds.

This suggests the use of the l_∞norm in segmentation of high-resolution images, which may be necessary in many practical cases; it can be an interesting tool in order to obtain more efficient results. It was evidenced, through an extensive experimentation using standard images, that the use of the l_∞ norm, instead of $l_2$norm, decreases the runtime of the mean shift when the values of bandwidths h_s and h_r increase. For more details on this issue see [Domínguez & Rodríguez, 2011].

Another application of our algorithm was in the medical image segmentation. It is of noticing that the mean shift can be considered as a segmentation unsupervised method. Unsupervised methods, which do not assume any prior scene knowledge which can be learned in order to help segmentation process, it are obviously more challenging than the supervised ones.

In order to have more clarity of the medical images that will be segmented, some details of the original images are given. Studied images were of arteries, which have atherosclerotic lesions and these were obtained from different parts of the human body. These arteries were contrasted with a special tint in order to accentuate the different lesions in arteries. The arteries were digitalized directly from the working desk via MADIP system with a resolution of 512x512x8 bit/pixels [Rodríguez et. al., 2001]. For more details on the characteristics of these images one can see [Rodríguez & Pacheco, 2007]. Another lesion type that were isolated is caused by disease of the visual system, glaucoma. "Glaucoma" is a term used for a group of diseases that can lead to damage to the optic nerve and result in blindness.

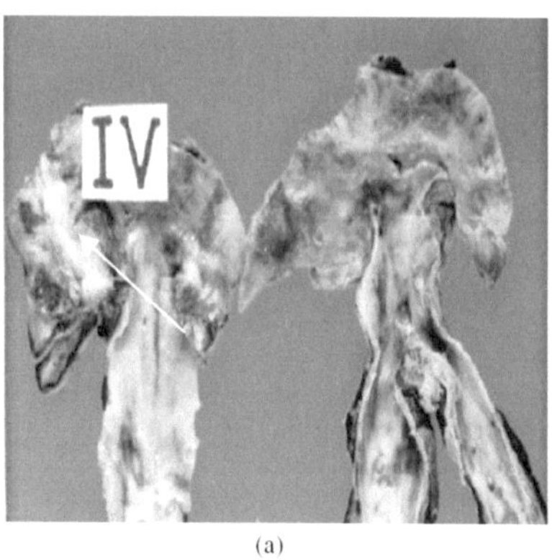

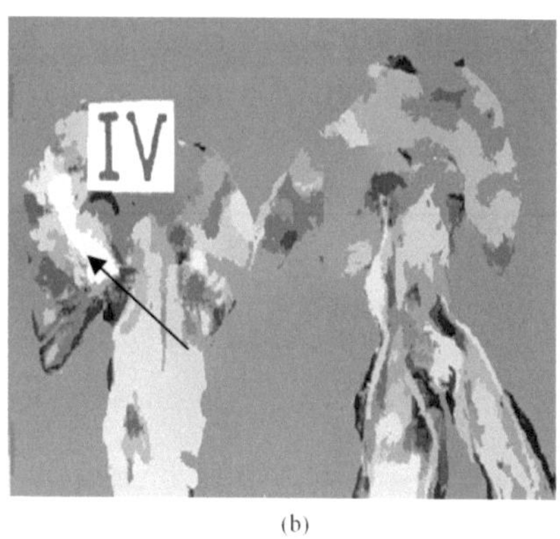

Figure 12. a) Original image, b) Unsupervised segmentation by using our algorithm. The arrows mark the isolated lesions.

In Figure 12, an example of segmentation on artery by using our algorithm is shown. Although another segmentation method was already applied to other atherosclerotic lesions

[Rodríguez & Pacheco, 2007]; here one can observe the obtained result when applying our unsupervised strategy.

In Figure 12, one can note that the lesion IV that appears in the original image was isolated (see arrows in Fig. 12 (a)). According to the criterion of physicians this is a good result, because the algorithm is able to isolate the lesion without any previous condition. Moreover, one also can see that the segmented image with the mean shift algorithm is totally free of noise. This is another important aspect when the mean shift filtering is used.

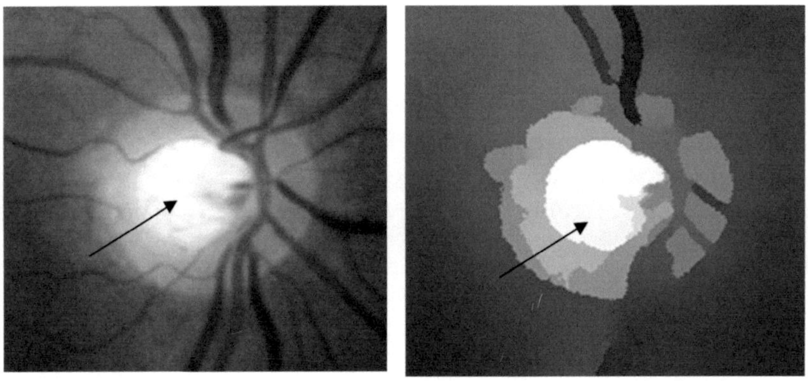

(a) (b)

Figure 13. a) Original image. b) Segmentation by using our unsupervised strategy. The arrow indicates the isolated lesion.

Another example is shown in Figure 13. In this case, the main objective is to isolate the oval from the vascular net of the eye (see arrow). This is of great importance for the study of the glaucoma disease. According to the criterions of physicians, the discrimination of this area is of great importance in order to know the advancement of the disease. In this case, this zone is isolated appropriately. A quantitative comparison of all the shown experimental results can be found in the presented references of the own authors [Rodríguez & Tovar, 2010].

Other issue of interest of the authors was to study the behaviour of the algorithm, taking into consideration the number of iterations and the degree of homogenization of the segmented images, for different values of the stopping threshold and window sizes. First, we go to analyze what happens when the values of the stopping threshold goes decreasing, and later on we will carry out an analysis when varying the window sizes.

The segmentation of the Astro's image for different values of the stopping threshold is shown in Figure 14. One can appreciate that the number of iterations increased in an abrupt way when the parameter *edsEnt* diminished from *0.001* to *0.0001*. However, from the point of view of a visual analysis a substantial change is not noticed in these segmented images (see Figures (f) and (g)). Homogenization is very similar. For such a reason in [Rodríguez et. al., 2012], a comparison through the XOR was carried out in order to better appreciate the difference among these images.

http://dx.doi.org/10.5772/50474

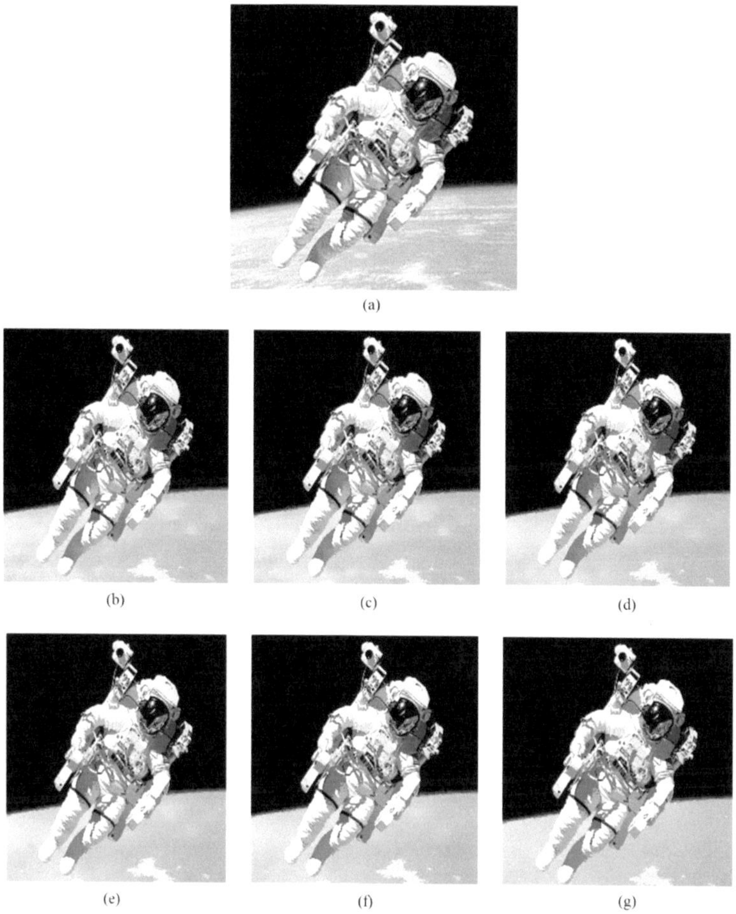

Figure 14. a) Original image (Astro), (b) Segmentation for *edsEnt* = *0.1,* 2 iterations, (c) Segmentation for *edsEnt* = *0.05,* 2 iterations, (d) Segmentation for *edsEnt* = *0.01,* 4 iterations, (e) Segmentation for *edsEnt* = *0.005,* 5 iterations, (f) Segmentation for *edsEnt* = *0.001,* 7 iterations, (g) Segmentation for edsEnt = *0.0001,* 60 iterations.

In this research, all the segmentation procedures were carried out by using a uniform kernel. We used the same window size in all the experiments (*hr* = *15, hs* = *4*), with the aim that the comparison of the obtained results was valid for different values of the stopping threshold (parameter *edsEn*).

One can observe that, in dependence on the image features the number of iterations varied and the same one has not a lineal behaviour. Figure 15, it presents the obtained segmentation results with the baboon's image. To observe, for example, that for *edsEnt* = *0.005* the image of Figure 14 (e) was obtained in 5 iterations, while for that same value, the image of Figure 15 (e) was attained in 14 iterations. This is due to the quantity of low or high frequencies of the original image. Note that, the image of Figure 14 is rich in low frequencies (this image has more homogeneous areas). Opposite happens with the image of Figure 15 (this image is rich in high frequencies).

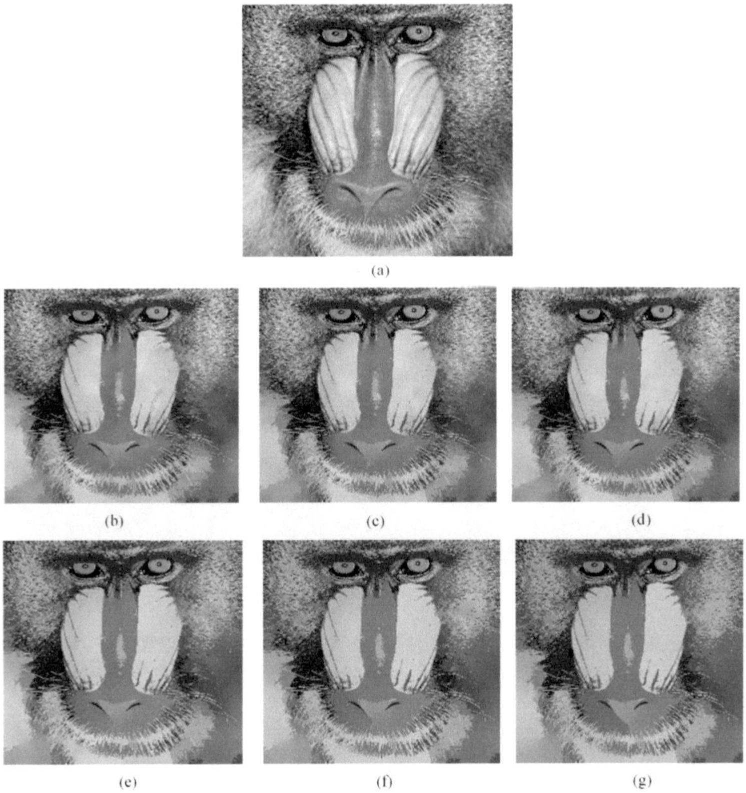

Figure 15. a) Original image (Baboon), (b) Segmentation for *edsEnt* = *0.1,* 2 iterations, (c) Segmentation for *edsEnt* = *0.05,* 3 iterations, (d) Segmentation for *edsEnt* = *0.01,* 5 iterations, (e) Segmentation for *edsEnt* = *0.005,* 14 iterations, (f) Segmentation for *edsEnt* = *0.001,* 27 iterations, (g) Segmentation for *edsEnt* = *0.0001,* 57 iterations.

Image	*EdsEnt*	*No. Iterac*	*EdsEnt*	*No. Iterac*	*EdsEnt*	*No. Iterac*
Astro	0.1	2	0.05	2	0.01	4
Baboon	0.1	2	0.05	3	0.01	5
Bird	0.1	2	0.05	2	0.01	3
Barbara	0.1	2	0.05	2	0.01	2
Image	***EdsEnt***	***No. Iterac***	***EdsEnt***	***No. Iterac***	***EdsEnt***	***No. Iterac***
Astro	0.005	5	0.001	7	0.0001	60
Baboon	0.005	14	0.001	27	0.0001	57
Bird	0.005	4	0.001	18	0.0001	19
Barbara	0.005	8	0.001	8	0.0001	42

Table 3. Values of the stopping threshold (*EdsEnt*) and number of iterations.

http://dx.doi.org/10.5772/50474

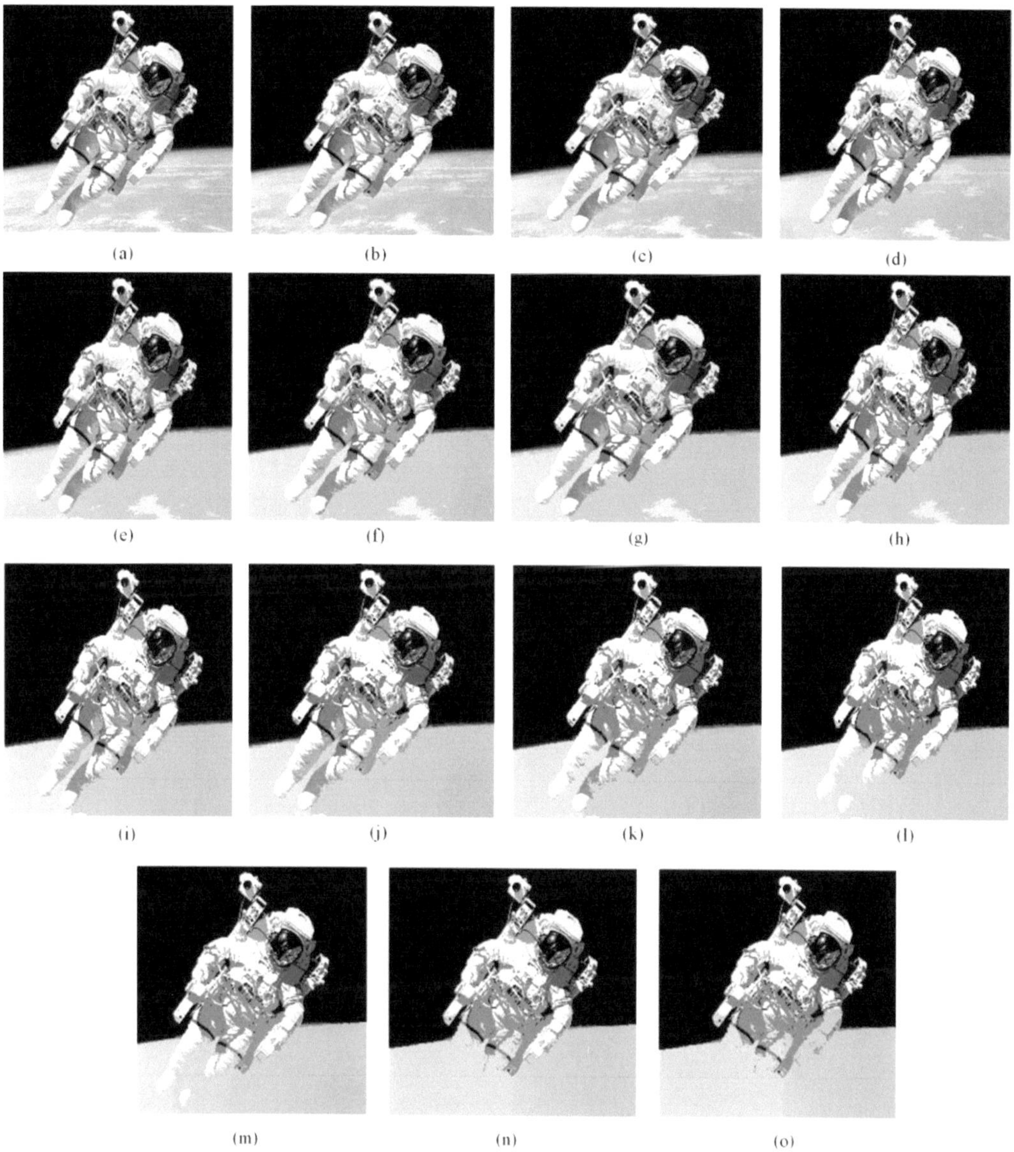

Figure 16. a) Original image (Astro), (b) Segmentation for *hr = 5* and *hs = 2,* 6 iterations, (c) Segmentation for *hr = 7* and *hs = 4,* 7 iterations, (d) Segmentation for *hr = 9* and *hs = 6, 12* iterations, (e) Segmentation for *hr = 11* and *hs = 8,* 65 iterations, (f) Segmentation for *hr = 13* and *hs = 10,* 70 iterations, (g) Segmentation for *hr = 15* and *hs = 12, 11* iterations, (h) Segmentation for *hr = 17* and *hs = 14,* 39 iterations, (i) Segmentation for *hr = 19* and *hs = 16,* 55 iterations, (j) Segmentation for *hr = 21* and *hs = 18, 7* iterations, (k) Segmentation for *hr = 23*and *hs = 20, 7* iterations, (l) Segmentation for *hr = 25* and *hs = 22, 37* iterations, (m) Segmentation for *hr = 27* and *hs = 24, 4* iterations, (n) Segmentation for *hr = 29* and *hs = 26, 23* iterations, (o) Segmentation for *hr = 31* and *hs = 28, 17* iterations. The arrow indicates the cloud permanency for that window size (image (h)).

It is necessary to point out that, for large values of the stopping threshold (*edsEnt*), the number of iterations had a very similar behaviour for images rich in low frequencies as well as for images rich in high frequencies (see Table 3 and Figures 14 and 15). On the other hand, one can appreciate that, in this image (see Figure 15), the number of iterations also increased abruptly when the stopping threshold was from *edsEnt* = *0.001* to *0.0001*. However, between the two images (see Figures 15 (f) and (g)), the difference is not visually appreciated. This appreciation was also analysed with more detail in [Rodríguez et. al., 2012].

This same study was carried out, fixing the value of stopping threshold, for different values of window sizes (parameters *hs* and *hr*). In this case the selected stopping threshold was *edsEn* = *0.001* (see algorithm *No. 1*). The segmentation of the Astro's image for different parameters *hr* and *hs*, in Figure 16 is represented.

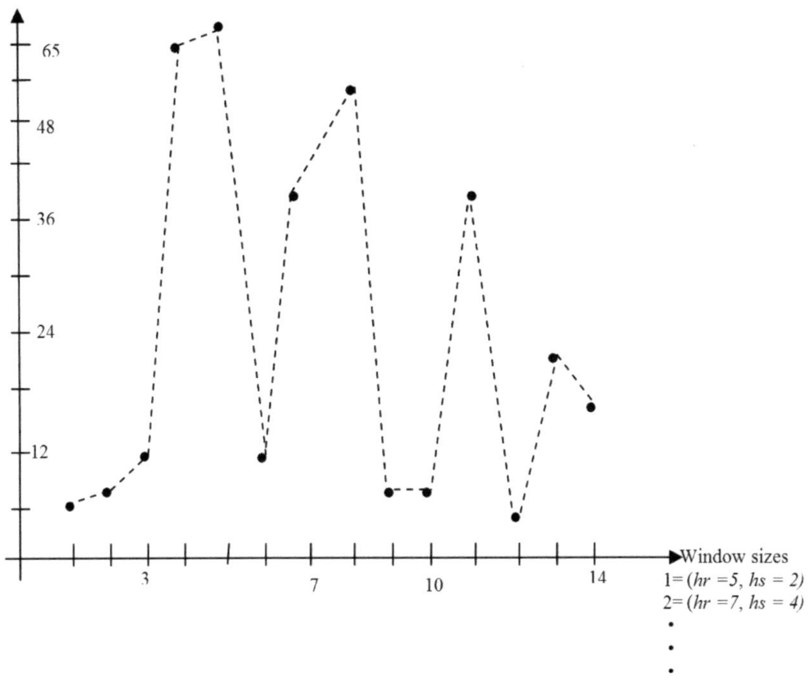

Figure 17. Graph that represents the number of iterations vs. the window sizes. Note the undulant behavior of the number of iterations with regard to the window sizes.

Some interesting comments arise of the obtained results that appear in Figure 16. Observe that, proportionally to the increase of the width of the radii *hr* and *hs*, the homogenization degree increased in the segmented image. However, the number of iterations had a behavior that fluctuated. In other words, the number of iterations did not increase lineally, in this image, when increased the radius *hr* and *hs*. Note that, in small radius the segmentation was very rude. One can observe that visually, homogeneous areas were not denoted with regard to the original image (see Figures 16 (b), (c) and (d)).

http://dx.doi.org/10.5772/50474

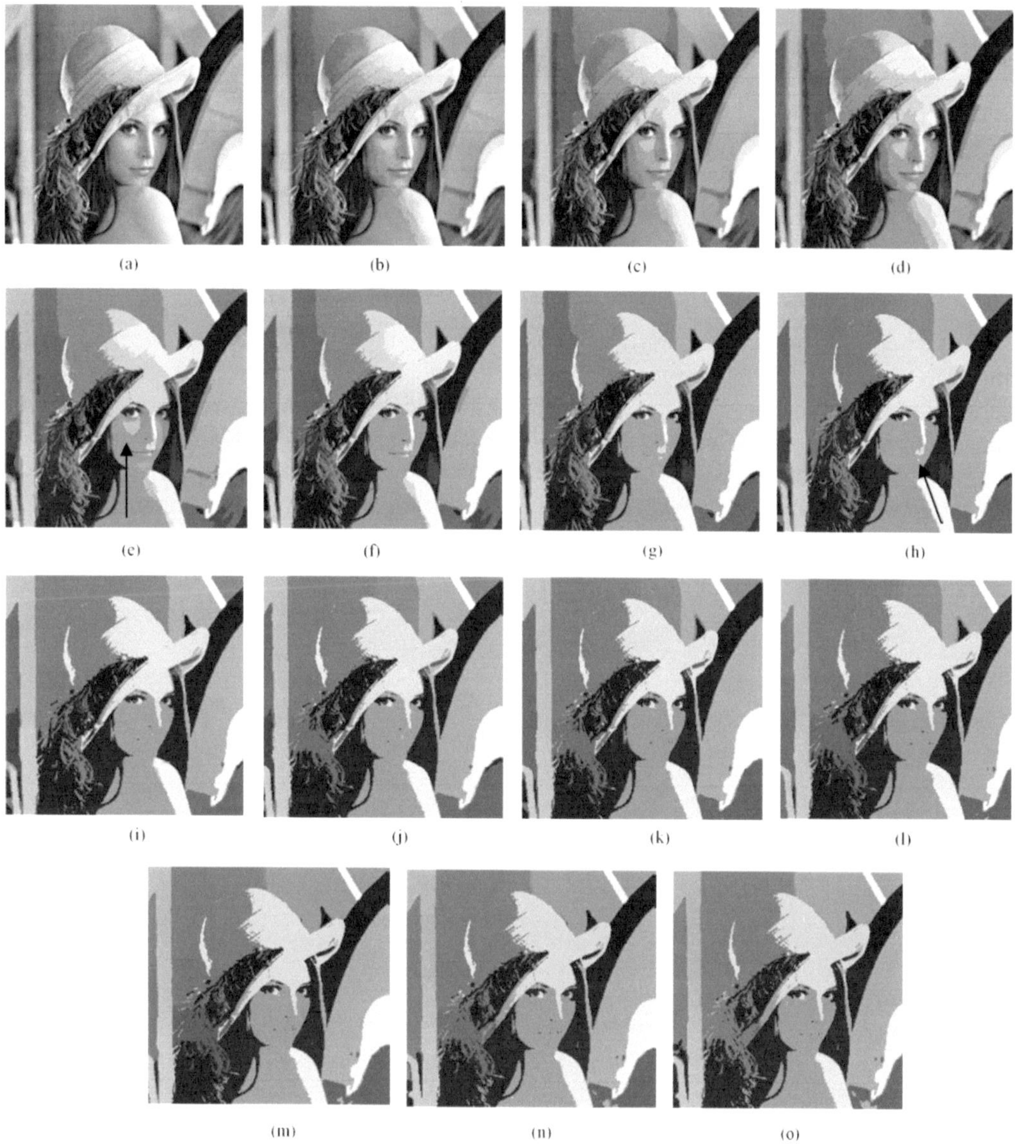

Figure 18. a) Original image (Lena), (b) Segmentation for *hr* = *5* and *hs* = *2, 14* iterations, (c) Segmentation for *hr* = *7* and *hs* = *4, 16* iterations, (d) Segmentation for *hr* = *9* and *hs* = *6, 25* iterations, (e) Segmentation for *hr* = *11* and *hs* = *8, 48* iterations, (f) Segmentation for *hr* = *13* and *hs* = *10, 25* iterations, (g) Segmentation for *hr* = *15* and *hs* = *12, 20* iterations, (h) Segmentation for *hr* = *17* and *hs* = *14, 26* iterations, (i) Segmentation for *hr* = *19* and *hs* = *16, 24* iterations, (j) Segmentation for *hr* = *21* and *hs* = *18, 21* iterations, (k) Segmentation for *hr* = *23*and *hs* = *20, 26* iterations, (l) Segmentation for *hr* = *25* and *hs* = *22, 13* iterations, (m) Segmentation for *hr* = *27* and *hs* = *24, 5* iterations, (n) Segmentation for *hr* = *29* and *hs* = *26, 8* iterations, (o) Segmentation for *hr* = *31* and *hs* = *28, 10* iterations. The arrows indicate the permanency of stains for those window sizes.

However, for window sizes very big the earth is totally homogeneous (see arrow in Fig. 16 (i)). In other words, starting from *hr* = *19* and *hs* = *16*, the earth in totally uniform (see Figures 16 (j), (k) and (l)). Moreover, one visually does not observe difference among these images. Alone, in the images of Figures (n), (m) and (o), the feet of the cosmonaut were combined with the gray level of the earth. In order to verify this visual impression, a comparison of these images through the *Xor* was carried out in [Rodríguez et. al., 2011b]. On the other hand, it is possible to see that, in all these segmented images (for big window sizes), the behavior of the number of iterations was also oscillating; that is, these did not grow proportionally when increased the window sizes (see Fig. 17).

Figure 18 shows the obtained results with the image of Lena. Observe in Figure 18 that, the same as in the previous example, proportionally to the increase of the width of the radius *hr* and *hs*, the degree of uniformity increased in the segmented images. However, in this case for small radii, contrary to the previous example, the numbers of iterations were bigger. The explanation of this behavior, it comes given by the characteristics of the original image (high frequencies in the image). On the other hand, the number of iterations in this example also had an oscillating behaviour, that is; these did not increase proportionally with the window sizes.

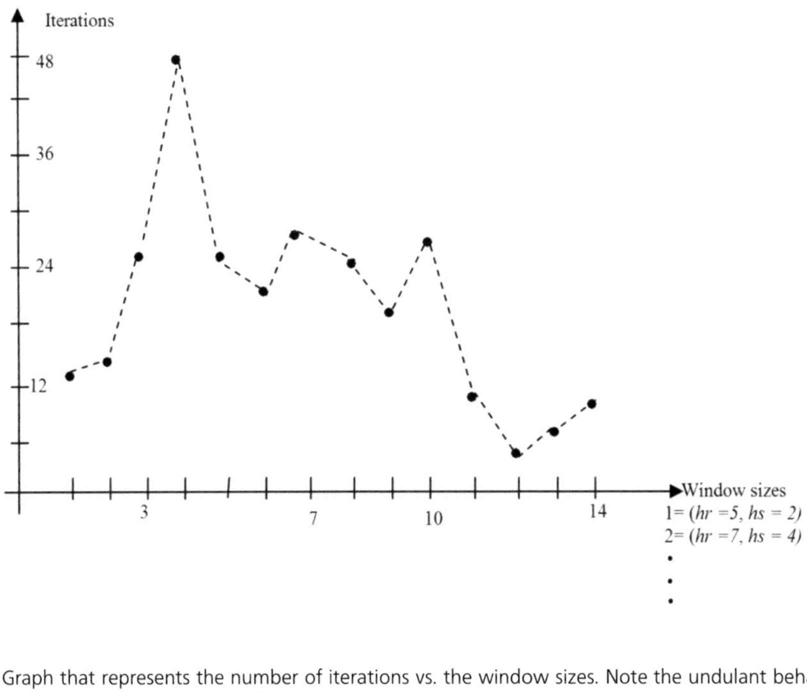

Figure 19. Graph that represents the number of iterations vs. the window sizes. Note the undulant behavior of the number of iterations with regard to the window sizes.

In this result, one can see that, starting from *hr* = *13* and *hs* = *10*, the face of woman begins to be uniform and the stain below of the left eye disappeared (see arrow in Fig. 18 (e)). Moreover, starting from *hr* = *19* and *hs* = *16*, the face of woman is totally uniform and the shade that is under the nose also disappears (see arrow in Fig. 18 (h)). Here also in these results the behavior of the number of iterations, in relation to the increase of the window sizes *hr* and *hs*, were oscillating; these did not grow proportionally when increased the window sizes (see Fig. 19).

By way of summary, in Table 4, the window sizes and the iteration numbers appear for each of the segmented images.

Astro(hr, hs)		No. Iter.	Lena (hr, hs)		No. Iter.
5	2	6	5	2	14
7	4	7	7	4	16
9	6	12	9	6	25
11	8	65	11	8	48
13	10	70	13	10	25
15	12	11	15	12	20
17	14	39	17	14	26
19	16	55	19	16	24
21	18	7	21	18	21
23	20	7	23	20	26
25	22	37	25	22	13
27	24	4	27	24	5
29	26	23	29	26	8
31	28	17	31	28	10

Table 4. Window sizes (*hr and hs*) and the iteration numbers.

Table 4, it offers a comparative panoramic vision of all the segmented images. Also, one can see the behaviour of the iteration numbers with regard to the window sizes. This behaviour can be explained via Figure 20. In Figure 20, the value of *hs* is related to the spatial resolution of the analysis while the value *hr* defines the range resolution. The spatial resolution *hs* has a different effect on the output image when compared to the gray level resolution (*hr, spatial range*). Only features with large spatial support are represented in the segmented image with our algorithm when *hs* is increased. On the other hand, only features with high contrast survive when *hr* is large. Then, as *2xhs* establishes the range of the movement spatially and in the range of *2xhr* is carried out an averaged; then the characteristics of image in this range (*2xhr*) will influence on this average (bigger quantity of low or high space frequencies). This issue is what produced the oscillation, in the iteration number, when varying the window sizes (*hr* and *hs*). In addition, it is necessary to point out that the iteration number did not have relationship some with the quality of the segmented image. For example, with small windows can be bigger the number of iterations that with big windows; however, it was observed that with small window sizes the segmentation was rude. A quantitative comparison of these results can be found in [Rodríguez et. al., 2011b].

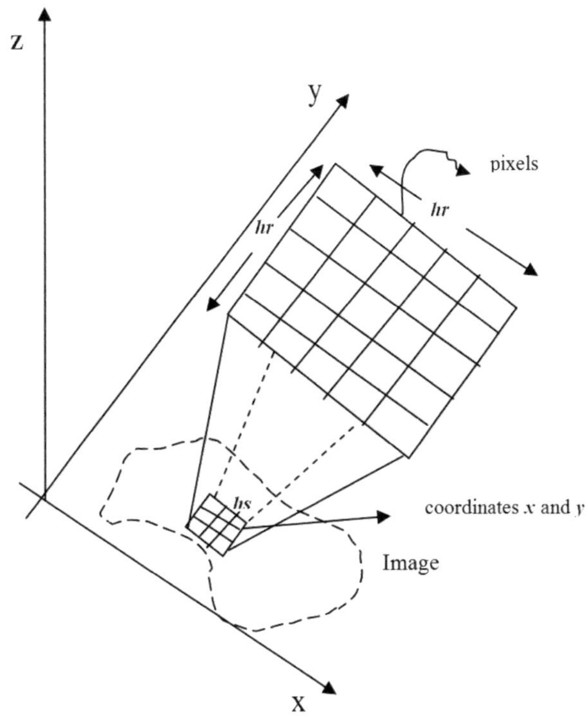

Figure 20. Graphic representation of the radius hr and *hs*. Movement through an image.

6.1. Some related philosophical issues with image segmentation

Segmentation is recognized to be one of the most important steps in most high-level image analysis systems. Its precise functioning highly determines the performance of the entire system. Image segmentation is today routinely used in a multitude of different applications, such as: medical diagnosis, treatment planning, robotics, pathology, geology, anatomical structure studies, meteorology and computer-integrated surgery, to mention a few. However, image segmentation remains a difficult task due to both the diversity of the object's shape and image's quality. In spite of the most elaborated algorithms developed until now, segmentation remains a very dependent procedure of the application. Until now any single method that can cope with all the problems that can be found does not exist and unfortunately, segmentation remains a complex problem with no exact solution.

For example, of the segmented images those appear in Figure16, which to select as the best segmented image? The answer to this question is not direct, because it depends on the aim of observer. If one wants, for example, a good segmentation of the sky and the earth, the segmented images of Figure 16 (m), (n) and (o), these would be the most appropriate. However, one can observe in these images that the feet of the astronaut are practically lost. Therefore, if the aim of observer was a good segmentation of the astronaut, these images (Figs. 16 (m), (n)) would not be the best selection. For this aim, the images chosen in Figure 16 would be those (i), (j) or (k). This corroborates that the segmentation is heavily dependent on the application. All this analysis, the reader could carry out it to the segmented images that in Figure 18 appear.

In those segmentation applications where one wants a binary image and the background and objects only should appear; for example, to count regions, the problem could be a little less complicated. An example of this issue is in the count of blood vessels (see Figure 8). Here, one is speaking of segmented images where the final result is a bit/pixel. The problem of segmentation begins to get complicated when the segmented image has several regions, more than 5, 6, 7, 8, 9, …… bit/pixel, and mainly when one is working with unsupervised segmentation strategies. In the measure that is bigger the number of bit/pixel of the segmented image, the segmentation problem is much more complicated. For example, in the case of supervised segmentation the number of bit/pixel (number of regions) is controlled by the observer and in many practical applications this segmentation method is not very problematic.

On the other hand, one should have in mind the features of the original image. In general, before that the segmentation process is carried out, the original image should be filtered through a low pass filter. In many practical applications this step is very important and many times the final result of segmentation depends on this step. When one uses the iterative algorithm of mean shift this step is implicit, because the mean shift itself is a low pass filter.

The election of one or another segmentation method depends on several factors, namely: a) on the knowledge that the observer has on the method, b) of the application in itself, c) of features of the original image, among others. A universal method of segmentation has not been created, due to that the world of images is practically infinite. For example, the interpretation that a pathologist makes from a biopsy image; which necessarily goes by a segmentation process, it is different to the interpretation that a radiologist makes from a radiological image. It is evident that both are different applications. One could continue analyzing the segmentation issue, but this is an open theme which it will need of many more iterations.

7. Conclusions

In this chapter, we carried out an introduction on theoretical aspects of the mean shift. We also introduced the idea of working with l_∞ norm and we proved that, of this way, one can obtain bigger homogenization degree. We proved the convergence of the mean shift by using the l_∞ norm.

The iterative algorithm that was used in this chapter, where entropy was utilized as a stopping criterion, it was presented too. Through an extensive experimentation by using real and standard images, we showed and we discussed the obtained results with our iterative algorithm. We proved that our algorithm can be used as an unsupervised suitable strategy to carry out complex problems of segmentation. Some application examples by using our algorithm were shown.

On the other hand, in order to prove the good performance of our algorithm, the same was compared with another segmentation algorithm established already. Through several experiments with real images, we proved that the segmented images by using our iterative algorithm were less noisy than those obtained by means of other methods.

Finally, some related philosophical themes with image segmentation were discussed.

Author details

Roberto Rodríguez Morales[1*], Didier Domínguez[1], Esley Torres[1] and Juan H. Sossa[2]

*Address all correspondence to: rrm@icimaf.cu

1 Institute of Cybernetics, Mathematics & Physics (ICIMAF), Digital Signal Processing Group, Cuba

2 National Polytechnic Institute (IPN), Computing Research Center, Mexico

References

[1] Cheng, Y. (1995). Mean Shift, Mode Seeking, and Clustering. *IEEE Trans., Pattern Analysis and Machine Intelligence*, 17(8), 790-799.

[2] Chenyang, X., Dzung, P., & Jerry, P. (2000). Image Segmentation Using Deformable Models. *SPIE Handbook on Medical Imaging, Medical Image Analysis. Edited by J. M. Fitzpatrick and M. Sonka*, III, Chapter 3, 129-174.

[3] Cheriet, M., Said, J. N., & Suen, C. Y. (1998). A Recursive Thresholding Technique for Image Segmentation. *IEEE Transactions on Image Processing*, 7(6).

[4] Chin-Hsing, C., Lee, J., Wang, J., & Mao, C. W. (1998, January). Colour image segmentation for bladder cancer diagnosis. *Mathematical and Computer Modelling*, 27(2), 103-120, 0895-7177.

[5] Christoudias, C. M., Georgescu, B., & Meer, P. (August 2002). Synergism in Low Level Vision. Quebec City, Canada. *16th International Conference on Pattern Recognition*, IV, 150-155.

[6] Comaniciu, D. I. (2000). Nonparametric Robust Method for Computer Vision. *Ph.D. Thesis*, New Brunswick, Rutgers, The State University of New Jersey.

[7] Comaniciu, D., & Meer, P. (2002, May). Mean Shift: A Robust Approach toward Feature Space Analysis. *IEEE Transaction on Pattern Analysis and Machine Intelligence*, 24(5), 0162-8828.

[8] Domínguez, D., & Rodríguez, R. (2009). Use of the L (infinity) norm for image segmentation through Mean Shift filtering. *International Journal of Imaging*, 2(S09), 81-93.

[9] Domínguez, D., & Rodríguez, R. (2011). Convergence of the Mean Shift using L (infinity) norm in image segmentation. *International Journal of Pattern Recognition Research* [1], 32-42.

[10] Fukunaga, K., & Hostetler, L. D. (1975, January). The Estimation of the Gradient of a Density Function. *IEEE Transactions on Information Theory* [1], IT-21, 32-40, 0018-9448.

[11] Grenier, T., Revol-Muller, C., Davignon, F., & Gimenez, G. (2006, 8-11, (Oct. 2006)). Hybrid Approach for Multiparametric Mean Shift Filtering, Image Processing. *IEEE, International Conference, Atlanta, GA*, 1541-1544.

[12] Kenong, W., Gauthier, D., & Levine, M. D. (1995, January). Live Cell Image Segmentation. *IEEE Transactions on Biomedical Engineering*, 42(1), 1-11, 0018-9294.

[13] Koss, J., Newman, F., Johnson, D., & Kirch, D. (1999, July). Abdominal organ segmentation using texture transforms and a hopfield neural network. *IEEE Transactions Medical Imaging*, 18(7), 0278-0062.

[14] Otsu, N. (1978). A threshold selection method from grey level histogram. *ILEE Trans. Systems Man Cybernet* [SMC-8], 62-66.

[15] Rodríguez, R., Alarcón, T., & Sánchez, L. (2001). MADIP: Morphometrical Analysis by Digital Image Processing. Spain. *Proceedings of the IX Spanish Symposium on Pattern Recognition and Image Analysis*, I, 291-298, 84-8021-349-3.

[16] Rodríguez, R., Alarcón, T., & Pacheco, O. (2005, October). A New Strategy to Obtain Robust Markers for Blood Vessels Segmentation by using the Watersheds Method. *Journal of Computers in Biology and Medicine*, 35(8), 665-686, 0010-4825.

[17] Rodríguez, R., & Suarez, A. G. (2006). An Image Segmentation Algorithm Using Iteratively the Mean Shift. *Book Series Lecture Notes in Computer Science*, Publisher Springer, Berlin/Heidelberg, 4225, *Book Progress in Pattern Recognition, Image Analysis and Applications*, 326-335.

[18] Rodríguez, R., & Pacheco, O. (2007). A Strategy for Atherosclerosis Image Segmentation by using Robust Markers. *Journal Intelligent & Robotic System*, 50(2), 121-140.

[19] Rodriguez, R. (2008). Binarization of medical images based on the recursive application of mean shift filtering: Another algorithm. *Journal of Advanced and Applications in Bioinformatics and Chemistry*, I, 1-12, Dove Medical Press Ltd.

[20] Rodríguez, R., & Tovar, R. (2010). An Unsupervised Strategy for Bio-medical Image Segmentation. *Journal of Advanced and Applications in Bioinformatics and Chemistry* [3], 67-73.

[21] Rodriguez, R., Suarez, A. G., & Sossa, J. H. (2011a). A Segmentation Algorithm based on an Iterative Computation of the Mean Shift Filtering. *Journal Intelligent & Robotic System*, 63(3-4), 447-463.

[22] Rodriguez, R., Torres, E., & Sossa, J. H. (2011b). Image Segmentation based on an Iterative Computation of the Mean Shift Filtering for different values of window sizes. *International Journal of Imaging and Robotics*, 6(A11), 1-19.

[23] Rodríguez, R., Torres, E., & Sossa, J. H. (2012). Image Segmentation via an Iterative Algorithm of the Mean Shift Filtering for Different Values of the Stopping Threshold. *International Journal of Imaging and Robotics*, 7(1).

[24] Salvatelli, A., Caropresi, J., Delrieux, C., Izaguirre, M. F., & Caso, V. (2007). Cellular Outline Segmentation using Fractal Estimators. Journal of Computer Science and Technology ., 7(1), 14-22.

[25] Shen, C., & Brooks, M. J. (2007, May). Fast Global Kernel Density Mode Seeking: Applications to Localozation and Tracking. *IEEE Transactions on Image Processing*, 16(5), 1457-1469, 1057-7149.

[26] Suyash P., Awate, & Ross T., Whitaker. (2006, March). Higher-Order Image Statistics for Unsupervised, Information-Theoretic, Adaptive, Image Filtering. *IEEE Trans. Pattern Analysis and Machine Intelligence (PAMI)*, 364-376, 28(3).

[27] Vicent, L., & Soille, P. (1991, June). Watersheds in digital spaces: An efficient algorithm based on immersion simulations. *IEEE Transactins on Pattern Analysis and Machine Intelligence*, 13(6), 583-593, 0162-8828.

[28] Zhang, H., Fritts, J. E., & Goldman, S. A. (2003). Paper presented at Proceeding of The SPIE. *A Entropy-based Objective Evaluation Method for Image Segmentation, Storage and Retrieval Methods and Applications for Multimedia 2004. Edited by Yeung, Minerva; Lienhart, M., Rainer W.; Li, Choung-Sheng*, 5307, 38-49.

Chapter 4

Constrained Compound MRF Model with Bi-Level Line Field for Color Image Segmentation

P. K. Nanda and Sucheta Panda

Additional information is available at the end of the chapter

http://dx.doi.org/10.5772/50475

1. Introduction

Image segmentation is a basic early vision problem which serves as precursor to many high level vision problems. Color image segmentation provides more information while solving high level vision problems such as, object recognition, shape analysis etc. Therefore, the problem of color image segmentation has been addressed more vigorously for more than one decade. Different color models such as RGB, HSV, YIQ, Ohta (I_1, I_2, I_3), CIE(XYZ, Luv, Lab) are used to represent different colors [5]. From the reported study, HSV and (I_1, I_2, I_3) have been extensively used for color image segmentation. Ohta color space is a very good approximation of the Karhunen-Loeve transformation of the RGB, and is very suitable for many image processing applications [1]. Image Modeling plays a crucial role in image analysis. Stochastic models, particularly MRF models, have been successfully used as the image model for image restoration and segmentation [2], [3], [4]. MRF model has also been successfully used as the image model while addressing the problem of color image segmentation both in supervised and unsupervised framework. Kato *et al* [6] have proposed a MRF model based unsupervised scheme for color image segmentation. In Kato 's method, the model parameters have been estimated using Maximum Likelihood criterion and the only parameter identified by the user is the number of class. This algorithm could be validated using different color textures and real images. Another color texture unsupervised segmentation algorithm has been proposed by Deng *et al* [7] and the method has been retermed as JSEG method. Recently, an unsupervised image segmentation algorithm has been proposed by Guo *et al* [8] where K-means has been used to initialize the classification in the classification of numbers. Very recently Scarpa *et al.* [13] have proposed a multiscale texture model and a related algorithm for the unsupervised segmentation of color images. In this scheme, the feature vectors have been collected and based on the feature vector the textures are then recursively merged giving rise to larger and more complex textures. This algorithm could successfully be tested on real world natural and remote sensing images. The model parameters can be estimated in both supervised and unsupervised framework [6].

In this piece of work, a Constrained Compound MRF model based color image segmentation scheme is proposed in unsupervised framework. We have used Ohta (I_1, I_2, I_3) color space to model the color images. In the proposed scheme, the Constrained Compound MRF model parameters and the image labels are estimated concurrently. Since the image label estimates and the estimates of model parameters are dependent on each other, obtaining global estimates of label as well as model parameters is very hard. Hence, we have proposed a recursive scheme for estimation of image labels and model parameters. The recursive scheme yields partial optimal solutions as opposed to optimal solutions. The MRF model parameter estimation problem is formulated in Maximum Conditional Pseudo Likelihood (MCPL) framework and the MCPL estimates are obtained using homotopy continuation bases algorithm. The MCPL estimation strategy results in a set of nonlinear equations which need to be solved to determine the model parameter estimates. Determination of the estimates is tantamount to determine the zeros of the unknown function. Homotopy continuation methods [14], [15] are globally convergent methods that have been used to trace the zeros of a function and hence determines the solution of functions. We have developed the fixed point based homotopy continuation method to estimate the model parameters. The image label estimation problem is formulated in Maximum a Posteriori (MAP) framework and the MAP estimates are obtained using the proposed hybrid algorithm [10]. The proposed supervised algorithm has been successfully tested on different images, however, for the sake of illustration we have presented three results and a comparison is made with [9].

2. MRF model

MRF theory is a branch of probability theory for analyzing the spatial or contextual dependencies of physical phenomena. It is used in visual labeling to establish probabilistic distributions of interacting labels.

2.1. Neighborhood system and cliques

The sites in S are related to one another via a neighborhood system. A neighborhood system for S is defined as

$$N = \{N_i \,/\, \forall i \in S\} \tag{1}$$

Where N_i is the set of sites neighboring i. The neighboring relationship has the following properties:

1. A site is not neighboring to itself: $i \in N_i$

2. The neighboring relationship is mutual: $i \in N_{i} \Leftrightarrow N_{i}$

$$N_i = \left\{ i' \in S / \left[dist\left((x_{i'}, y_{i'}), (x_i, y_i) \right) \right]^2 \le r, i' \ne i \right. \tag{2}$$

For a regular lattice S, the set of neighbors of i is defined as the set of sites within a radius of $\sqrt{r}$ from i.

Where dist (A, B) denotes the Euclidean distance between A and B and r takes an integer value. The Fig 1 shows (η^1) the first order and second order neighborhood system (η^2).

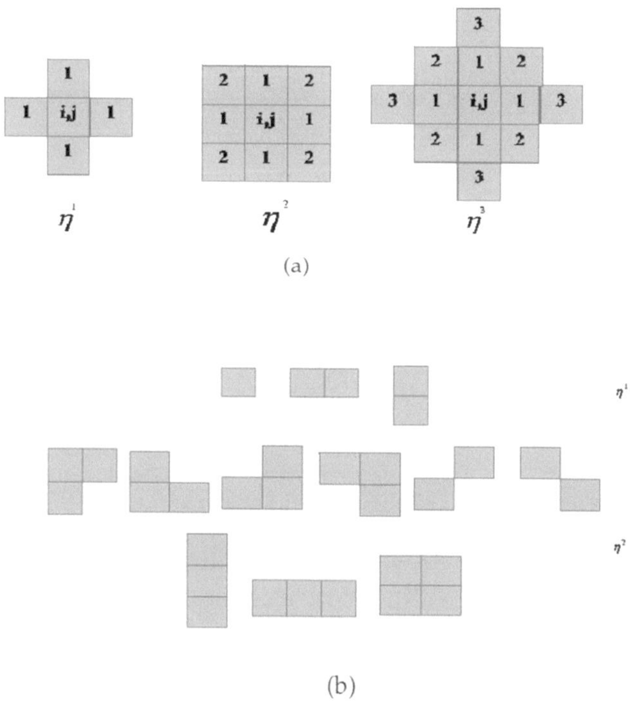

Figure 1. (a) Figure showing first order (η^1), second order (η^2) and third order(η^3)neighborhood structure (b) Cliques on a lattice of regular sites.

The pair (S, N) = G constitutes a graph in the usual sense; s contains the nodes and N determines the links between the nodes according to the neighboring relationship. A clique c for (s, N) is defined as a subset of sites c={i, i'), or a triple of neighboring sites c = {i, i', i''), and so on. The collections of single-site, pair-site and triple-site cliques will be denoted by C_1, C2, and C3 respectively, where

$$C_1 = \{ i / i \in S \} \tag{3}$$

$$C_2=\{\{i,i'\}/i' \in N_i, i \in S\} \tag{4}$$

$$C_3=\{\{i,i',i''\}/i,i',i'' \in S \text{ are neighbors to one another}\} \tag{5}$$

The sites in a clique are ordered, and {i, i'} is not the same clique as {i', i}, and so on. The collection of all cliques for (S, N) is

$$C=C_1 \cup C_2 \cup C_3 \cup ..... \tag{6}$$

The type of a clique for (S, N) of a regular lattice is detetrmined by its size, shape and orientation. Fig. 1 shows the clique types for the first order and second order neighborhood systems for a lattice [2] [3].

Let $Z = \{Z_1, Z_2, ..., Z_m\}$ be a family of random variables defined on the set S, in which each random variable Z_i takes a value z_i in L. The family Z is called a random field. We use the notion $Z_i = z_i$ to denote the event that Z_i takes the value z_i and the notion $(Z_1 = z_1, Z_2 = z_2, ..., Z_m = z_m)$.

To denote the joint event. For simplicity a joint event is abbreviated as Z = z where $z = \{z_1, z_2, ...\}$ is a configuration of z, corresponding to realization of a field. For a discrete label set L. the probability that random variable Z_i takes the value z_i is denoted $P(Z_i = z_i)$, abbreviated $P(z_i)$ and the joint probability is denoted as $P(Z=z) = P(Z_1 = z_1, Z_2 = z_2, ..., Z_m = z_m)$ and abbreviated P(z).

F is said to be a Markov Random Field on S with respect to a neighborhood system N if and only if the following two conditions are satisfied:

$$P(Z=z)>0, \forall z \in Z \qquad (Positivity) \tag{7}$$

$$P(z_i / z_{S-i}) = P(z_i / z_{N_i}) \qquad (Markovianity) \tag{8}$$

Where S-i is the set difference, z_{S-I} denotes the set of labels at the sites in S-i and

$$z_{N_i}=\{z_{i'} / i' \in N_i\} \tag{9}$$

Stands for the set of labels at the sites neighboring i.

The positivity is assumed for some technical reasons and can usually be satisfied in practice. The Markovianity depicts the local characteristics of Z. In MRF, only neighboring labels have direct interactions with each other[2][3].

http://dx.doi.org/10.5772/50475

The concept of MRF is a generalization of that of Markov processes (MPs) which are widely used in sequence analyisis. An MP is defined on a domain of time rather than space. It is a sequence of random variables Z_1, Z_2, ..., Z_m defined in the time indices 1, 2, ..., m. It is generalized into MRFs when the time indices are considered as spaial indices.

3. Compound Markov Random Field (COMRF) model

Capturing salient spatial properties of an image lead to the development of image models. MRF theory provides a convenient and consistent way to model context dependent entities for e.g. image pixels and correlated features [6]. Though the MRF model takes into account the local spatial interactions, it has its limitations in modeling natural scenes of distinct regions. In case of color models, it is known that there is a correlation among the color components of RGB model. In our formulation, we have decorrelated the color components and introduced an interaction process to improve the segmentation accuracy. We have employed inter-color-plane interaction (Ohta I_1, I_2, I_3 color model) process which reinforces partial correlation among different color components.

In this work, a compound MRF model has been proposed and the proposed model is based on the following notion. The prior MRF model takes care of (i)Intra-color-plane I_1 *or* I_2 *or* I_3 I_1, I_2, *and* I_3 entities of each color plane(ii)Inter-color-plane interactions of pixels of different color planes for e.g. I_1 *and* I_2, *and* I_3. The MRF prior model takes care of the spatial interactions in any given color plane and also interaction of a pixel of a given color plane with the pixel of other color planes. Thus the intra color plane and inter color plane interactions could be modeled by the compound MRF model. Motivation behind this modeling is as follows. It is known that strong correlation exists among different color planes of RGB model and therefore not suitable for image segmentation. On the other hand Ohta model is suitable for image segmentation because of the existing weak correlation among color planes. In order to develop an appropriate color model, we develop a model with controlled correlation among the different color planes. Therefore, the a prior compound MRF model takes care of the controlled correlation among the different planes of Ohta colorspace. The degree of correlation is controlled by the associated parameters of the clique potential function I_1, I_2, I_3. The values of these parameters are quite low and hence provide a controlled weak correlation among the inter planes making it suitable for image segmentation.

We assume all images to be defined on discrete rectangular lattice MxN. In the following the Compound MRF model is developed. Let the observed image X be modeled as a random field and x is a realization which is the given image. Let Z denote the label process associated with the segmented image Fig.2(a) shows the three planes of Ohta color model. Each color plane is modeled by a MRF model. Let L denote the number of labels. For a given plane for example Z, if the spatial interactions are modeled by MRF, then the prior probability distribution $P(Z)$ is Gibbs distributed and can be expressed as

$$P\left(Z^1 = z^1 \middle| \theta\right) = \left(1/z'\right)e^{-U\left(z^1,\theta\right)} \tag{10}$$

where $Z' = \sum_{z'} e^{-U(z',\theta)}$ is the partition function, $U(z^1, \theta)$ is the energy function and is of the form $U(z', \theta) = \sum_{c \in C} V_c(z', \theta)$ being referred to as cliqe potential function, θ denotes the clique parameter vector. Analogously the spatial interactions of I_2 and I_3 planes can be defined. This prior MRF model taking care of all the three spatial planes would result in the energy function of the following form

$$\begin{aligned} &P\left(Z = z \middle| \theta\right) = \left(1/z'\right)e^{-U(z,\theta)} \\ &z' = \sum_z e^{-U(z,\theta)} \\ &U(z,\theta) = \sum_{c \in C} V_c(z,\theta) \end{aligned} \tag{11}$$

where, $V_c(z, \theta)$ denotes the clique potential function for the three spatial planes I_1, I_2 and I_3 respectively. However, the model is not complete for the color model. We model Z as a compound MRF, where the spatial interactions of individual color planes are taken care together with the inter color plane interactions of pixels. The inter color plane interactions of pixels of one plane with the other is shown in Fig.1(a). For the sake of illustration, Fig.1(b) shows interaction of (i, j) $^{(th)}$ pixel of I_2 plane with the pixels of I_1 plane with the first order neighbourhood structure in the inter color plane direction. If this inter color plane interactions need to modeled with the MRF prior, we can express

$$P(Z^{I_2}_{i,j} = z^{I_2}_{i,j} / Z^{I_1}_{k,l} z^{I_1}_{k,l}, (k, l) \in I_1) =$$
$$P(Z^{I_2}_{i,j} = z^{I_2}_{i,j} / Z^{I_1}_{k,l} = z^{I_1}_{k,l}, (k, l) \neq (i, j), (k, l) \in \eta^{I_1}_{i,j})$$

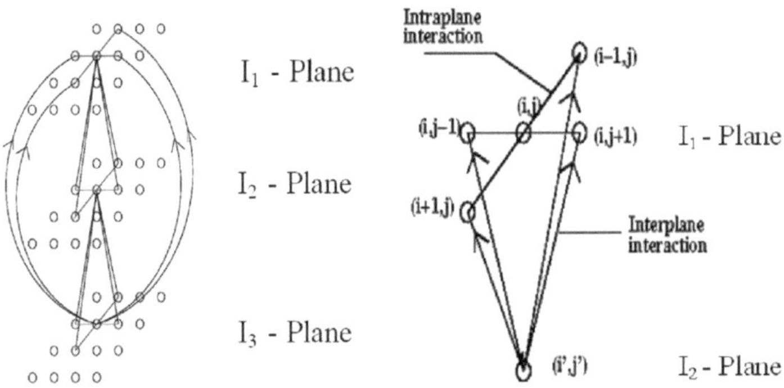

Figure 2. (a) I1, I_2, I_3 Plane Interaction (b) Interaction of one pixel of I_1 –plane with I_2 -plane.

Let z denote the labels of pixels taking care of all three color planes. In otherwords, z denotes the labels for pixels of the color image. For example, $z_{\{i,\ j\}}$ corresponds to the (i, j) th pixel label consisting of three color components. The prior probability of z has been contributed by the intra color plane interactions and inter color plane interactions of pixels. hence, the prior model of z consists of the clique potential functions $V_{cs}(z)$ and $V_{ct}(z)$ corresponding to intra color plane interactions and inter color plane interactions respectively. The vertical and horizontal line fields for different color planes (k=1, 2, 3) are denoted as $v^{\{k\}}$ and $h^{\{k\}}$ respectively. The horizontal and vertical line fields are defined as follows. Let $f_v\left(z^k_{i,j}, z^k_{i,j-1}\right)$ for the kth color plane be defined as $f_v\left(z^k_{i,j}, z^k i,\ j-1\right)=\left|z^k_{i,j}-z^k_{i-1,j}\right|$ $f_h\left(z^k_{i,j}, z^k_{i,j-1}\right)>threshold$. Vertical line field for each plane is set i.e.

$v_{\{i,\ j\}}{}^{\{k\}}=1$ for k=1, 2, 3, if $f_v\left(z^k_{i,j}, z^k_{i,j-1}\right)>threshold$, else $v_{\{i,\ j\}}{}^{\{k\}}=0$. Similarly, in case of horizontal line field let $f_h\left(z^k_{i-1,j}, z^k_{i,j}\right)$ be defined as $f_h\left(z^k_{i,j}, z^k i,\ j-1\right)=\left|z^k_{i,j}-z^k_{i-1,j}\right|$.

Horizontal line field for k th plane is set, i.e. $h_{\{i,\ j\}}{}^{\{k\}}=1$ for k=1, 2, 3, if else $h_{\{i,\ j\}}{}^{\{k\}}=1$. Since the compound MRF model takes care of intra color plane as well as inter color plane interactions the prior probability distribution is given by (10), where the energy function can be expressed as,

$$U(z,\theta)=U_s(z,\theta)+U_t(z,\theta) \tag{12}$$

Where,

$$U_s(z,\theta)=\sum_{i,j}V_{c_s}(z,\theta) \tag{13}$$

$$U_t(z,\theta)=\sum_{i,j}V_{c_t}(z,\theta) \tag{14}$$

Here, $U_s(z,\ \theta)$ and $U_t(z,\ \theta)$ refers to the energy function of intra-color-plane and inter-color-plane respectively. $V_{cs}\ (z_{i,\ j})$ corresponds to the intra-color-plane pixels and $V_{ct}\ (z_{i,\ j})$ corresponds to inter-color-plane pixels. Let h_s^k for k=1, 2, 3 denote the horizontal line field for each color plane in intra-color-plane and h_t^k for k=1, 2, 3 denote the vertical line fields for inter-color-plane directions. Thus the compound MRF model will have the energy function given by (12). Equation (13) can be written as,

$$\begin{aligned}V_{c_s}\left(z_{i,j}\right)=&\sum_{k=1}^{3}\alpha^k\left[\left(z^k_{i,j}-z^k_{i,j-1}\right)^2\left(1-v^k_{i,j}\right)+\left(z^k_{i,j}-z^k_{i-1,j}\right)^2\left(1-h^k_{i,j}\right)\right]\\&+\beta^k\left[v_{i,j}+h_{i,j}\right]\end{aligned} \tag{15}$$

Here, z^1, z^2, z^3 correspond to I_1, I_2, I_3 planes respectively. The equation (14) can be written as,

$$\begin{aligned}V_{c_t}(z_{i,j}) &= \alpha^1\left[\left(z^1_{i,j}-z^2_{i,j-1}\right)^2\left(1-v^1_{i,j}\right)+\left(z^1_{i,j}-z^2_{i,j-1}\right)^2\left(1-h^1_{i,j}\right)\right]+\beta^1\left[v^1_{i,j}+h^1_{i,j}\right]\\ &+\alpha^2\left[\left(z^2_{i,j}-z^3_{i,j-1}\right)^2\left(1-v^2_{i,j}\right)+\left(z^2_{i,j}-z^3_{i,j-1}\right)^2\left(1-h^2_{i,j}\right)\right]+\beta^2\left[v^2_{i,j}+h^2_{i,j}\right]\\ &+\alpha^3\left[\left(z^3_{i,j}-z^1_{i,j-1}\right)^2\left(1-v^3_{i,j}\right)+\left(z^3_{i,j}-z^1_{i,j-1}\right)^2\left(1-h^3_{i,j}\right)\right]+\beta^3\left[v^3_{i,j}+h^3_{i,j}\right]\end{aligned} \tag{16}$$

Where z^1 denotes the interaction between I_1-I_2 color planes, z^2 denotes the interaction between I_2-I_3 color planes and z^3 denotes the interaction between I_3-I_1 color planes respectively. Here we have assumed, $\alpha_1=\alpha_2=\alpha_3=\alpha$ and $\beta_1=\beta_2=\beta_3=\beta$. The $[\alpha, \beta]^T$ is the set of unknown parameter vector that are selected on *ad hoc* basis. Since the line fields correspond to the edge pixels and in turn the boundary of a given segment. The similarity measure in case of boundary pixels for k=1, 2, 3 is not required and hence for boundary pixels, i.e. when $h_{i,j}=1$ and $v_{i,j}=1$, for k=1, 2, 3 the clique potential function of (16) consists of only the penalty function. Therefore the boundary pixels should not participate in the formation of regions with similarity measure.

4. Constrained Markov Random Field (MRF) model

In probability theory, a martingale is a stochastic process (i.e., a sequence of random variables) such that the conditional expected value of an observation at some time t, given all the observations up to some earlier time s, is equal to the observation at that earlier time s. Precise definitions are given below.

Originally, martingale referred to a class of betting strategies popular during 18th century, in France. The simplest of these strategies was designed for a game in which the gambler wins his stake if a coin comes up heads and loses it if the coin comes up tails. The strategy had the gambler double his bet after every loss, so that the first win would recover all previous losses plus win a profit equal to the original stake. Since as a gambler's wealth and available time jointly approach infinity his probability of eventually flipping heads approaches 1. The martingale betting strategy was seen as a sure thing by those who practiced it. Of course in reality the exponential growth of the bets would eventually bankrupt those foolish enough to use the martingale for a long time. The concept of martingale in probability theory was introduced by Paul Pierre LÃ©vy, and much of the original development of the theory was done by Joseph Leo Doob. Part of the motivation for that work was to show the impossibility of successful betting strategies.

A discrete-time martingale is a discrete-time stochastic process (i.e., a sequence of random variables X_1, X_2, X_3 that satisfies for all n,

$$E(|X_n|)<\infty$$

$$E(X_{n+1}/X_1, X_2, X_3, \ldots, X_n) = X_n$$

i.e., the conditional expected value of the next observation, given all of the past bservations, is equal to the last observation.

Capturing the salient spatial properties of an image lead to the development of image models [3]. Though the MRF model takes into account the local spatial interactions, it has its limitations in modeling natural scenes of distinct regions. In order to incorporate a stronger local dependence, we constrain this model based on the notion of martingale.The motivation behind the new model is as follows.

MRF model takes care of the local spatial interactions, nevertheless it has limitation in modeling natural scenes. In the following we propose new model with a view to take care of intra as well as inter plane interactions. In this research work, we employed the notion of martingale to reinforce the local dependence. Let $Z(i)$, $i=1, 2, ...n$ be a martingale sequence, namely for all $i=1, 2, ...n$ $E[\mid Z(n)\mid]<\infty$

and $E[Z(n+1)/Z(1), ...Z(n)]=Z(n)$. Now, let $Z_1, Z_2, ...Z_n$ be the random variables associated with the image of size $n=N^2$ and G is the predefined number of class labels. Therefore, $E[Z_{i,j}/Z_{k,l}, k, l\neq i, j]=Z_{i-1,j}$ for any $k, l\in\eta_{i,j}$, where $\eta_{i,j}$ is the neighborhood of i, j. Consider,

$$E\left[Z_{i,j}\mid Z_{k,l},k,l\neq i,j\right]=\sum_{z_{i,j}\in L} z_{i,j}P\left[Z_{i,j}=z_{i,j}\mid Z_{k,l}=z_{k,l},k,l\neq i,j\right] \tag{17}$$

Assuming further that Z is a Markov process, we have

$$E\left[Z_{i,j}\mid Z_{k,l},k,l\neq i,j\right]=\sum_{z_{i,j}\in L} z_{i,j}P[Z_{i,j}=z_{i,j}/Z_{k,l}=z_{k,l},k,l\in\eta_{i,j}]$$
$$\sum_{z_{i,j}\in L} z_{i,j}\frac{P(Z=z)}{\sum_{z_{i,j}\in L}P(Z=z)} \tag{18}$$

Since Z is a MRF,

$$E\left[Z_{i,j}\mid Z_{k,l},k,l\neq i,j\right]=\sum_{z_{i,j}\in L} z_{i,j}\frac{P(Z=z)}{\sum_{z_{i,j}\in L}P(Z=z)} \tag{19}$$

Since $Z_{i,j}$ is a martingle sequence $E[Z_{i,j}\mid Z_{k,l}, k, l\neq i, j]=z_{k,l}\ \forall\ k, l\in\eta_{i,j}$

$$z_{k,l},k,l\in\eta_{i,j}=\sum_{z_{i,j}\in L} z_{i,j}\frac{e^{-U(z)}}{\sum_{z_{i,j}\in L}e^{-U(z)}} \tag{20}$$

Considering first order neighbourhood and choosing one of the neighbourhood pixels for example $z_{i-1,j}$, equation(20) can be expressed as

$$z_{i-1,j} = \sum_{z_{i,j} \in L} z_{i,j} \frac{e^{-U(z)}}{\sum_{z_{i,j} \in L} e^{-U(z)}}$$

Instead of taking a given pixel from the neighbourhood $z_{i-1,j}$, we take the average of the neighborhood pixels. The *a priori* model of Z takes care of this constraint and the $U(Z)$ is modified as (for $\forall$ (i, j))

$$U(z) = \sum_{i,j} U(z_{i,j}) + \lambda_c \{z_{i,j_{avg}} - \sum_{z_{i,j} \in L} z_{i,j} \frac{e^{-U(z)}}{\sum_{z_{i,j} \in L} e^{-U(z)}}\}^2 \tag{21}$$

Where $z_{i,j_{avg}} = \sum_{z_{i,j} \in L} z_{i,j} \frac{e^{-U(z)}}{\sum_{z_{i,j} \in L} e^{-U(z)}}$ and λ_c is the constrained model parameter. The energy function consists of two terms

$$U(z) = \sum_{c \in C_{in}} V_c(z_s^1, z_s^2, z_s^3) + \sum_{c \in C_{ir}} V_c(z_t^1, z_t^2, z_t^3) \tag{22}$$

Where $V_c(z_s^1, z_s^2, z_s^3)$ and $V_c(z_t^1, z_t^2, z_t^3)$ are given by (15) and (16) respectively.

4.1. Constrained Compound Markov Random Field (CCMRF) model

The notions of the Constrained model has been fused with the notion of Compound Model to develop a new model known as Constrained Compound Model [10].

The model is given by

$$U_{sc}(Z) = \sum_{i,j} U(z_{i,j}) + \lambda_c \left\{ z_{i,j_{avg}} - \sum_{z_{i,j} \in L} z_{i,j} \frac{e^{-U(z_{i,j})}}{\sum_{z_{i,j} \in L} e^{-U(z_{i,j})}} \right\}^2 \tag{23}$$

Where,

$$U_{sc}(Z) = V_{c_s}(z_{i,j}) + \lambda_c \left\{ z_{i,j_{avg}} - \sum_{z_{i,j} \in L} z_{i,j} \frac{e^{-U(z_{i,j})}}{\sum_{z_{i,j} \in L} e^{-U(z_{i,j})}} \right\} \tag{24}$$

Where U_{sc} denote the energy function corresponding to intra color plane interactions and $V_{cs}(z_{i,j})$ is defined by (15). Where, $Z_{i,j_{avg}} = \sum_{z_{i,j} \in L} z_{i,j} \frac{e^{-U(z_{i,j})}}{\sum_{z_{i,j} \in L} e^{-U(z_{i,j})}}$ and λ_c is the constrained model parameter. The energy function taking care of both intra-color-plane and inter-color-plane interactions with intra plane constraints is given by

$$U(Z) = U_{s_c}\left(z_{i,j},\theta\right) + U_{t_c}\left(z_{i,j},\theta\right) \tag{25}$$

Where $U_{s_c}(z_{i,j}, \theta)$ is defined by (24) and $U_{t_c}(z_{i,j}, \theta)$ is defined by (14).

$V_{c_s}(z_{i,j})$ and $V_{c_t}(z_{i,j})$ are given by (15) and (16) respectively.

5. Unsupervised framework

In unsupervised scheme, the MAP estimates of the labels and the estimates of the model parameters are carried out concurrently. Thus, an estimation strategy need to be developed, which using the observed image, X, will yield an optimal pair (Z^{opt}, θ^{opt}). The following joint optimality criterion is considered,

$$\left(z^{opt},\theta^{opt}\right) = \arg_{z,\theta} \max P\left(Z = z \middle| X = x,\theta\right) \tag{26}$$

The estimated pair satisfying (26) is the global optima of P(Z=z/X=x, θ) with respect to Z and θ. Since both the entities Z and θ are unknown, and interdependent the problem is a very hard problem. Therefore, it is necessary to opt for strategies for suboptimal solution. In (26), z, θcould be viewed as a set of parameter of the given function P(Z=z/X=x, θ). For such kind of problems in deterministic framework, Wendell and Horter have proposed an alternate approach that would yield suboptimal solutions instead of optimal solution. Their approach is based on splitting the variables followed by recursively estimating the parameters. The final estimate in this process is called as the partial optimal solution. In our case, in stochastic framework, we in the same spirit venture to split the original problem into estimation of labels (z) and parameters estimate θ to obtain the partial optimal solutions. The splitting of the variables can be expressed as follows

$$\left(z^*\right) = \arg_z \max P\left(Z = z \middle| X = x,\theta^*\right) \tag{27}$$

$$\left(\theta^*\right) = \arg_\theta \max P\left(Z = z^* \middle| X = x.\theta^*\right) \tag{28}$$

These partial optimal solutions Z *and θ^* are not global maxima, rather they are almost always local optimal solutions. But with θ=θ^*, the estimate z* is global optimal satisfying equation (27) and analogously for z=z*, θ^* is global optimal satisfying equation (28). Since neither θ^* nor z* is known, a recursive scheme is adopted where the model parameter estimation and segmentation is alternated. Let at the kth iteration $\theta^k = [\alpha^k, \varphi^k]^T$ be the estimate of model parameters and z^k be the estimate of the labels of the observed image. We adopt the following recursion

$$\left(z^{k+1}\right) = \arg_z \max P\left(Z = z \middle| X = x.\theta^k\right) \tag{29}$$

$$\left(\theta^{k+1}\right) = \arg_\theta \max P\left(Z = z^{k+1} \middle| X = x, \theta^*\right) \tag{30}$$

The first problem of equation (29) is solved using Bayesian approach [2]. The optimal value of θ^k is obtained by the proposed Homotopy Continuation method [6]. The MAP estimates are obtained by the proposed hybrid algorithm. One estimate of z^k and θ^k constitute one combined iteration. this recursion is continued for finite number of steps to obtain z^k and θ^k. Thus, the partial optimal solutions are obtained.

6. Image label estimation

The segmentation problem is cast as the pixel labeling problem. Each pixel can assume a label from the set of labels {0 – L}. In a given image of size L = M1 x M2, let $Z_{i,j}$ denote the random variable for (i, j)th pixel, ∀ (i, j) ϵ L = M1 x M2. Z denotes the label process and z denotes a realization of the process. The label estimates $\hat{z}$ is obtained by maximizing the posterior probability $P(Z = z \mid X = x, \theta)$. Thus, the optimality criterion can be expressed as follows,

$$\hat{z} = \arg_z \max P\left(Z = z \middle| X = x.\hat{\theta}\right) \tag{31}$$

where, θ denotes the associated parameter vector of the double MRF model Z. Since z is unknown the above equation can not be computed. So, by using Baye's theorem, hence (31) can be expre ssed as

$$\hat{z} = \arg_z \max \frac{P\left(X = x \middle| Z = z, \theta\right) P\left(Z = z\right)}{P\left(X = x \middle| \theta\right)} \tag{32}$$

The observed image X is given and hence the denominator $P(X = x \mid \theta)$ of (32) is a constant quantity. P(Z = z) is the *a priori* probability distribution of the labels. The degradation process is assumed to be Gaussian and hence $P(X = x \mid Z = z, \theta)$ of (32) can be written as $P(X = x \mid Z = z, \theta) = P(X = z + w \mid Z, \theta) = P(W = x - z \mid Z, \theta)$. Since, W is a Gaussian process, and there are three spectral components present in a color image, we have,

$$P\left(W = x - z \middle| Z, \theta\right) = \frac{1}{\sqrt{(2\pi)^n \det\left[\bar{K}\right]}} \quad -\frac{1}{2}(x-z)^T \bar{K}^{-1}(x-z) \tag{33}$$

Where K is the covariance matrix. Hence, this minimization can be expressed as,

$$\hat{z} = \arg_z \min \sum_{i,j} \sum_{k=1}^{3} \frac{\left(x^{(i)} - z^{(i)}\right)^2}{2\sigma^2} + v_{c_s}\left(z^k{}_{i,j}\right) + v_{c_t}\left(z^k{}_{i,j}\right) \tag{34}$$

$V_{c_s}(z_{i,j})$ and $V_{c_t}(z_{i,j})$ are given by (15) and (16) respectively. Solving (34) yields the MAP estimates of the image labels and hence segmentation. The color image has three spectral components x^k, z^k, k=1, 2, 3, V_c is the clique potential function for all the three spectral components.

7. Model parameter estimation

We estimate the *a priori* model parameter using the ground truth image z. The associated MRF parameters of this ground truth image is θ. We also assume the number of labels associated with the original image to be known. The parameter estimation problem is formulated using Maximum Likelihood criterion. Here the image label available at the (k+1)th iteration is used to estimate θ at (k+1)th iteration. Therefore, the problem can be stated as the following

$$\varphi^{k+1} = \arg\max P(Z = z^{k+1} / \theta) \tag{35}$$

Since, Z is a MRF, we have,

$$\varphi^{k+1} = \arg\max_{\theta} \frac{\exp(-U(z^{k+1}, \theta))}{\sum_{\zeta} \exp(-U(\zeta, \theta))} \tag{36}$$

where ζ ranges over all realizations of the image z. Because of the denominator of (36), computation of the joint probability $P(Z=z^{k+1}/\theta)$ is extremely difficult task. We maximize the pseudolikelihood function $\hat{P}(Z=z^{k+1}/\theta)$ instead of the likelihood function $P(Z=z/\theta)$ where

$$\prod_{(i,j)\in L} P(Z_{i,j}=z_{i,j}^{k+1}/Z_{m,n}=z_{m,n}^{k+1},(m,n)\in\eta_{i,j},\theta)=P(Z=z^{k+1}/\theta) \tag{37}$$

From the definition of marginal conditional probability, we can write

$$\prod_{(i,j)\in L} P(Z_{i,j}=z_{i,j}^{k+1}/Z_{k,l}=z_{k,l}^{k+1},(k,l)\neq(i,j),\forall(i,j)\in L,\theta) = \frac{P(Z=z^{k+1}/\theta)}{\sum_{z_{i,j}\in M} P(X=x/\theta)} \tag{38}$$

Because of MRF assumption,

$$\prod_{(i,j)\in L} P(Z_{i,j}=z_{i,j}^{k+1}/Z_{m,n}=z_{m,n}^{k+1},m,n\in\eta_{i,j},\theta) = \frac{\exp(-\sum_{c\in C} V_c(z^{k+1},\theta))}{\sum_{z_{i,j}\in M}\sum_{c\in C} V_c(z^{k+1},\theta)} \tag{39}$$

Substituting equation (39) in (37) we have

$$\hat{P}(Z=z^{k+1}/\theta) \approx \frac{\exp(-\sum_{c\in C} V_c(z^{k+1},\theta))}{\sum_{z_{i,j}\in M} \exp(V_c(z^{k+1},\theta))} \tag{40}$$

Therefore, the maximization problem (41) reduces to

$$\arg\max_{\theta} \hat{P}(Z=z^{k+1}/\theta) = \arg\max \prod_{(i,j)\in L} \frac{\exp(-\sum_{c\in C} V_c(z^{k+1},\theta))}{\sum_{z_{i,j}\in M} \exp(-\sum_{c\in C} V_c(z^{k+1},\theta))} \tag{41}$$

In (41), the summation is over all possible labels M. (41) is highly nonlinear in nature and no a priori knowledge of the solution is available. Solving the resulting non-linear equations is hard and hence we developed a globally convergent based Homotopy Continuation method. We carry out the maximization process and obtain the estimate of parameter vector θ with the help of homotopy continuation method based algorithm.

7.1. Salient steps of the unsupervised algorithm

1. Initialize parameter vector as θ^0, pixel label estimates z^0 for k=0, 1, 2, ..., N do

2. Using θ^k, observed image x and initial segmented image z^k, obtain the MAP estimate of the labels $\hat{z}^{k+1}$

3. With $\hat{z}^{k+1}$, obtain the MCPL estimate of the parameter vector $\hat{\theta}^{k+1}$, using homotopy continuation based algorithm

4. Compare $\hat{\theta}^{k+1}$ with the previous estimate of $\hat{\theta}^k$, if $|\hat{\theta}^{k+1} - \hat{\theta}^k| < threshold$, set $\theta^{k+1} = \theta^k$ go to step 2 else go to step 5

5. Set estimate of parameter vector $\theta^* = \hat{\theta}^{k+1}$

6. Estimate z^* (segmented image) using θ^*, $\hat{z}^{k+1}$ and observed image x

8. Parameter estimation using homotopy continuation method

8.1. Homotopy continuation method

Often, a wide variety of practical problems reduces to finding solution to a system of non-linear equations. The problem becomes difficult when we have little knowledge about the solutions of the system. In such situations, the popular Newton algorithm may fail to converge to a solution. Such examples can be found in [19]. Therefore, we need a method which, irrespective of the starting point always converges to a solution of the given system of equations. Homotopy continuation methods under some conditions always converges to a solution with probability one. Such methods are called globally convergent homotopy continuation methods [14]. The homotopy function is defined as follows :Let X, Y be two topological spaces and I be the unit interval $\lambda / 0 \leq \lambda \leq 1$. The two maps f, g be maps from a space X to a space Y $f, g : X \rightarrow Y$, then f is said to be homotopic to g if there exists a map $H : X \rightarrow Y$ such that H(x, 0) = f(x) and H(x, 1) = g(x) for $x \in [0, 1]$, such a map H is called a homotopy from f to g. In the above definition, H represents a continuous deformation of the map f to g as the parameter λ is varied from 0 to 1. There is no unique homotopy map that will continuously deform from a trivial map to any map. Depending upon the problem at hand the path has to be accurately tracked and hence, a suitable homotopy function has to be chosen for the existence of a path leading to the solution. The commonly used Homotopy maps are (i) Linear Homtopy (ii) Newton Homotopy (iii) Fixed Point Homotopy.

It is clear from Section 7 that the parameter estimation problem has been reduced to maximization of (41) with respect to θ. Towards this end let

$$f(\theta)=\frac{\partial}{\partial\theta}\{\log[\hat{P}(X=x^{k+1}/Y=y,\theta)]\} \tag{42}$$

Now the homotopy method is employed to solve $f(\theta)=0$. In the following, we develop a general framework for solving $f(\theta)=0$ using homotopy continuation method where θ is the unknown parameter vector to be determined.

In the continuation method we need to trace the homotopy path from a solution of a known system to that of the desired solution. In this regard, we have considered the fixed point homotopy map [14] which offers the advantage of arbitrary starting point for the path. This fixed point map is given by

$$h(\theta,\lambda,q)=\lambda f(\theta)+(1-\lambda)(\theta-q) \tag{43}$$

where $0\le\lambda\le1$ and q is an arbitrary starting point. Here the predictor-corrector method is employed to track the path defined by the homotopy in (43). The procedure can be briefly outlined as follows:

Let $(\theta^k,\lambda^k,\theta^{k-1})$ be a point that satisfies (43). Therefore, the point considered is on the path. Tracking the path involves computing the adjacent point on the path. This is determined in the following way. Increment λ^k by some small value $\Delta\lambda$ thus giving the next point $\lambda^{k+1}=\lambda^k+\Delta\lambda$ and evaluate equation (43) at $(\theta^k,\lambda^{k+1},\theta^{k-1})$. If the value of the map $h(\theta^k,\lambda^{k+1},\theta^{k-1})$ is not equal to zero, then the point $(\theta^k,\lambda^{k+1},\theta^{k-1})$ is not on the path. Since$h(\theta^k,\lambda^{k+1},\theta^{k-1})\neq0$, we try to obtain an estimate of θ^k, say $\hat{\theta}^k$ corresponding to λ^{k+1} such that $h(\theta^k,\lambda^{k+1},\theta^{k-1})\approx0$. To achieve this one could use Newton's algorithm, namely,

$$\hat{\theta}^k_{i+1}=\hat{\theta}^k_i-J^{-1}_{\hat{\theta}}[h(\hat{\theta}^k_i,\lambda^{k+1},\theta^{k-1})]h(\hat{\theta}^k_i,\lambda^{k+1},\theta^{k-1}) \tag{44}$$

Where the superscript i denotes the ith Newton iteration and is the inverse of the Jacobian of h with respect to the coefficient of the parameter vector θ. But if $\hat{\theta}_0{}^k$ is too far from $\hat{\theta}^k$ the value which makes, $h(\hat{\theta}^k,\lambda^{k+1},\theta^{k-1})\approx0$ then (44) may not converge. To improve the convergence of (44), we select the initial point as $\hat{\theta}_0{}^k=\theta^k$. A further improvement in the convergence is obtained by considering

$$\hat{\theta}^k_0=\hat{\theta}^k-\Delta\lambda J^{-1}_{\hat{\theta}}[h(\theta^k,\lambda^{k+1},\theta^{k-1})]\frac{\partial h}{\partial\lambda}h(\theta^k,\lambda^{k+1},\theta^{k-1}) \tag{45}$$

The derivation of (45) is analogous to the derivation of Stonick and Alexander [15] for our homotopy map (43). Equation (45) corresponds to the prediction of the next point by taking a step in the direction of the path's slope. For the fixed point homotopy map considered, (45) becomes

$$\hat{\theta}_0^k = \theta^k - \Delta\lambda\{\frac{I}{1-(\lambda^k+\Delta\lambda)} - \frac{I}{(1-(\lambda^k+\Delta\lambda))^2}$$
$$[\frac{F_\theta^{-1}(\theta^k)}{(\lambda^k+\Delta\lambda)} + \frac{I}{1-(\lambda^k+\Delta\lambda)}]^{-1}\}\{f(\theta^k) - (\theta^k - \theta^{k-1})\} \tag{46}$$

Where I is the identity matrix. The intermediate steps for arriving at (46) is given in [16] and [17]. If $\hat{\theta}_0{}^k$ estimated by (45) is not on the path then it is taken as the initial point in the correction step (44). Otherwise $\hat{\theta}_0{}^k$ is considered as the next point on the path. Suppose $|\hat{\theta}_{M+1}{}^k - \hat{\theta}_M{}^k| \leq \gamma$ then we set $\hat{\theta}_M{}^k = \hat{\theta}^k = \theta^{k+1}$.

8.2. Homotopy continuation algorithm

Initialize: ($\theta = \theta^0$ *and* $\lambda = 0$)

do{

Increment $\lambda^{k+1} = \lambda^k + \Delta\lambda$

Update θ^k to $\hat{\theta}_0{}^k$ using equation (38)

if ()

else

take $\theta_0{}^k$ the initial point for Newton algorithm

Update:

$\hat{\theta}_i{}^k$ *to* $\hat{\theta}_{k+1}{}^k$ using (40)

if ()

else go to update: }

(Until $\lambda = 1$).

9. Results and discussions

In simulation, two images with weak edges and two images having both weak as well as strong edges have been considered. The first original image, a liver image with ill defined edges, is shown in Fig. 3(a). In order to compute the percentage of misclassification error, the Ground Truth image, as shown in Fig. 3(b), has been constructed manually. The estimated MRF model parameters are, α= 0.005601, β = 2.34 and σ = 0.55. However σ is chosen by trial and error and is fixed at 0.5. The Percentage of Misclassification Error (PME) with respect to Ground Truth image is defined as PME = {number of misclassified pixels in all the classes}/{total number of pixels of the image}. The MAP estimates in each recursion has been obtained by our proposed hybrid algorithm [10]. The results obtained by basic MRF model is shown in Fig. 3(c), where it is observed that one of the weaker edge could be preserved while the ill defined edge adjacent to it is completely lost. In case of the CMRF model, some portions could be sharper but the adjacent ill defined edge could not be recovered as shown in Fig. 3(d). However, as seen from Fig. 3(e), the use of the proposed CCMRF model could preserve well the weak edge as well as the adjacent ill defined edges. In case of Yu 's [9] approach, the inside weak edge could not be preserved even though the outer edge could be preserved. The adjacent ill defined edge is completely lost as seen in Fig. 3(f). Thus, the proposed CCMRF model with bi-level line field with Gaussain weighted penalty function could preserve well the ill defined edges together with strong edges.

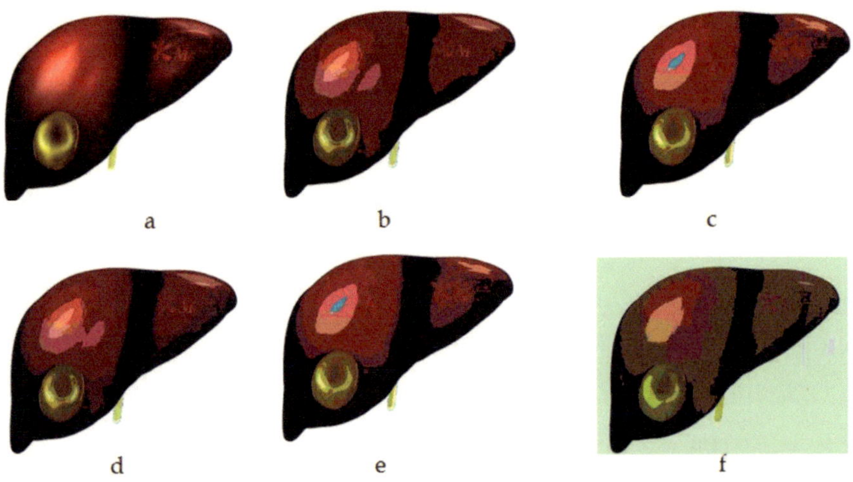

Figure 3. (a) Liver Abscess image (468x345) (b) Ground Truth (c) MRF optimized using Hybrid (d) CMRF optimized using Hybrid (e) CCMRF optimized using Hybrid (f) Clausi's result.

Fig.4(a) shows a cell image where the outer boundary of the cell is a strong edge while the inner portion of the cell contains weak edge or poorly defined edge. In order to compute the classification error, the corresponding ground truth image is manually constructed and is shown in Fig.4(b) and Fig.4(c) shows the result obtained with MRF model and it may be observed that the strong edges could be preserved but the weak edges could not be preserved. The poorly defined edges improved with CMRF model as shown in Fig.4(d). With CCMRF model, as observed from Fig.4(e), the outer edges of the cells could be preserved and the edges inside the different cells also have been well defined. The threshold considered for weak and strong edges are 0.91 and 0.25 respectively. The degradation process parameter is chosen to be 0.5 and the value k of the edge penalty function is chosen to be 0.2. This has also reflected in the misclassification error that is the PME is 22.72 for MRF model which reduced to 14.86 for CMRF model and further reduced to 3.11 for CCMRF model. As seen from Fig.4(f) Yu 's method preserved both weak and strong edges. The PME for Yu 's method is 6.21. It is found that the CCMRF model with bi-level line field proved to be the most effective among other methods.

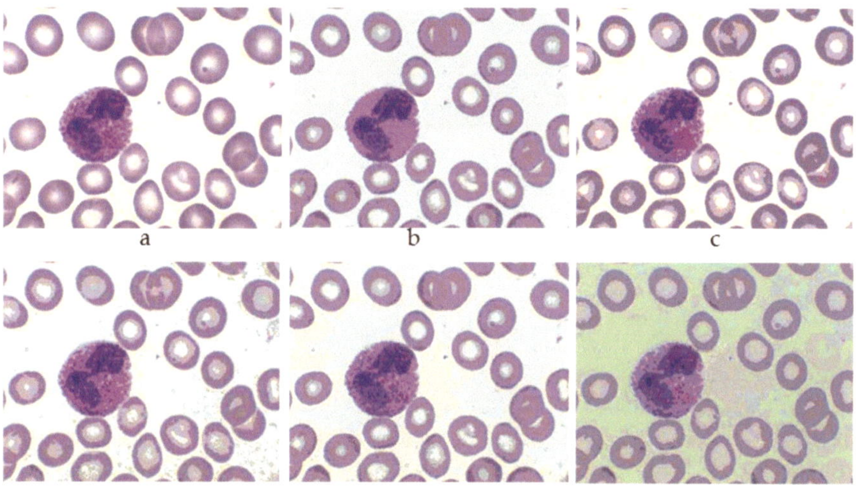

a b c

d e f

Figure 4. (a) Cell image (491x370) (b) Ground Truth (c) MRF optimized using Hybrid (d) CMRF optimized using Hybrid (e) CCMRF optimized using Hybrid (f) Clausi's result.

In order to demonstrate the unifying modeling property of the CMRF and CCMRF model, a third example as shown in Fig. 5(a) is considered where the background has texture like attributes. The estimated MRF model parameters are α = 0.01842, β= 2.79 and σ = 0.42. As observed from Fig.5(e) that the CCMRF model could segment the image and preserved many poorly defined edges. This observation is absent in case of use of the MRF and CMRF model. Use of CCMRF model could preseve the sharp features while Yu 's method could not preseve all the weak edges. This is observed from Fig. 5(f). The percentage of misclassification error also reflect the observation. Thus, in case of all the three examples, the use of CCMRF model could segment the image and preserve both the strong as well as weak edges. This proposed model could perform better than that of Yu 's approach [9] in the context of weak edge preservation and hence misclassfication error.

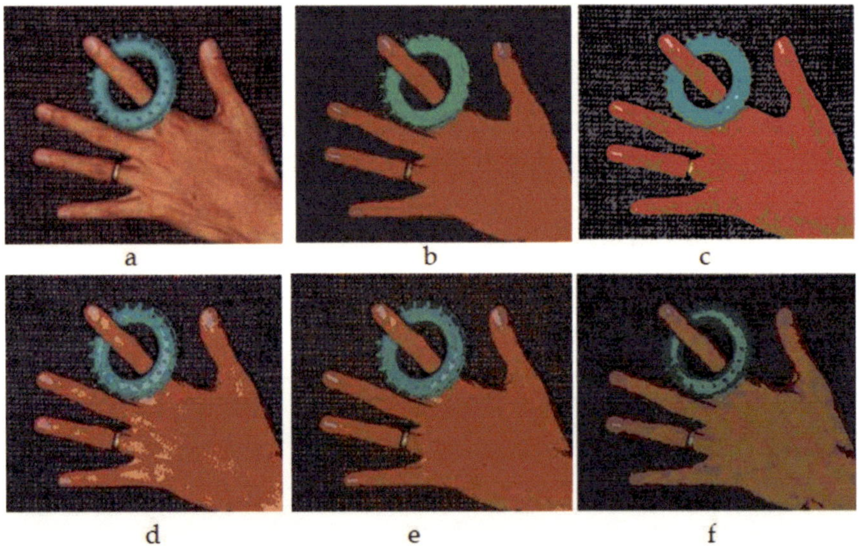

Figure 5. (a) Hand Ring (Indoor) image (303x243) (b) Ground Truth (c) MRF optimized using Hybrid (d) CMRF optimize dusing Hybrid (e) CCMRF optimize dusing Hybrid (f) Clausi'sresult.

Figure 6. (a) MANASA SOROVER (Remote Sensing) image (500x500) (b) Ground Truth (c) MRF optimized using Hybrid (d) CMRF optimized using Hybrid (e) CCMRF optimized using Hybrid (f) Clausi's result.

Similar observations have also been made in case of the Manasa Sorover image as shown in Fig.6(a). As observed from Fig.6(a) there are many weak edges to be preserved. In this case,

http://dx.doi.org/10.5772/50475

the CCMRF model with bi-level linefield could preserve many weak edges together with the strong edges. This may be seen from Fig.6(e) and it can be observed from Fig.6(d) that many weak edges have been preserved even using CCMRF model. Thus, in this example the performance of CCMRF model is found to be better than that of CMRF model in the context of misclassification error.

Acknowledgment

Our sincere thanks for anonymous reviewers for accepting this chapter.

Author details

P. K. Nanda[1] and Sucheta Panda[2*]

*Address all correspondence to: pandasucheta06@gmail.com

1 Department of Electronics and Comm. Engg., I.T.E.R, Siksha 'O' Anusandhan University, Orissa, India

2 Dept. of Computer Science & Engg., Padmanava College of Engg., India

References

[1] Y. I. Ohta, T. Kanade, T. Sakai.: "Color information for region segmentation." *Comp. Grap. Image. Process.*, vol 62, pp. 222-241, 1980.

[2] S. Geman, D. Geman.: "Stochastic relaxation, Gibbs distributions and the Bayesian restoration of images." *IEEE. Tranaction. PAMI*, vol 6, pp.721—741, 1984.

[3] S.Z.Li, *Markov Random Field modeling in computer vision*, Springer, Berlin, 1995.

[4] J. Besag: "On the statistical analysis of dirty pictures", J.Roy. Statist.Soc.B. 62, 1986, pp.259-302

[5] H. D. Cheng, X. H. Jiang, Y. Sun, Wang.J.: "Color Image Segmentation: Advances and prospects." *Pattern. Recog.*, vol 34, pp. 2259-2281, 2001.

[6] Z. Kato, T. C. Pong, J.C>M Lee, .: "Color image segmentation and parameter estimation in a morkovian framework". *Pattern Recognition Letters, vol.22, pp309-321, 2001.*

[7] Y. Deng, B. S. Manjunath, : "Unsupervised Segmentation of Color-Texture Regions in Images and Video". IEEE Transactions on Pattern Analysis and Machine Intelligence, vol. 23, no. 8, pp.800-810, 2001.

[8] L.Guo, Y.M.HouandX.M.Lun, An unsupervised color image segmentation algorithm based on context information *Pattern Recognition and Artificial Intelligence* vol.21, pp. 82-87, 2008.

[9] Qiyao Yu and David A. Clausi, "IRGS: Image Segmentation Using Edge Penalties and Region Merging, "*IEEE Transaction on Pattern Analysis and Machine Intelligence PAMI*, vol. 30, no. 12, pp.2126-2139, 2008.

[10] Sucheta Panda and P. K. Nanda, Constrained compound Markov Random field model with graduated penalty function for color Image Segmentation, *IEEE International conference on Control, Robotics and Cybernetics(ICCRC-2011)*, pp.VI-126-VI-132, 2011.

[11] C. Cheng, A. Koschan, C. H. Chen, D. L. Page and M. A. Abidi, Outdoor Scene Image Segmentation Based on Background Recognition and Perceptual Organization. *IEEE Transactions on Image Processing*, vol.21, no.3, pp.1007-1019, March2012.

[12] A. K. Mishra, P. W. Fieguth, D. A. Clausi. Decoupled Active Contour (DAC) for Boundary Detection. *IEEE Transactions on Pattern Analysis And Machine Intelligence*, vol.33, no. 5, pp.917-930, 2011.

[13] G. Scarpa, R. Gaetano, M. Haindl and J. Zerubia, Hierarchical multiple Markov chain model for unsupervised texture segmentation *IEEE Transactions on Image Processing* vol.18, pp.1830-1843, 2009.

[14] N. Chow, J. Mallet-Paret and J. A. Yorke, Finding zeros of maps: homotopy methods that are constructive with probability one, *Math.computation*, vol.32, no.143, pp. 887-899, 1978.

[15] V. L. Stonick and S. T. Alexander, A Relationship between recursive least square update and homotopy continuation methods, *IEEE Trans. Signal Processing*, vol.39, no.2, pp. 530-532, 1991.

[16] P. K. Nanda, K. Sunil Kumar, Sameer Gokhale and U. B. Desai, A multiresolution approach to color image restoration and parameter estimation using homotopy continuation method, *Proc. IEEE Int. Conf. on Image Proc.*, Washington, D. C, USA, Oct. 1995.

[17] P. K. Nanda, K. Sunil Kumar, Sameer Gokhale and U. B. Desai, A multiresolution approach to color image restoration and parameter estimation using homotopy continuation method, *Proc. IEEE Int. Conf. on Image Processing*, Washington, D.C, USA, vol 2, 45-48 Oct.1995.

Chapter 5

Cognitive and Statistical Pattern Recognition Applied in Color and Texture Segmentation for Natural Scenes

Luciano Cássio Lulio, Mário Luiz Tronco,
Arthur José Vieira Porto,
Carlos Roberto Valêncio and
Rogéria Cristiane Gratão de Souza

Additional information is available at the end of the chapter

http://dx.doi.org/10.5772/51862

1. Introduction

In this approach, cognitive and statistical classifiers were implemented in order to verify the estimated and chosen regions on unstructured environments images. As inspection of crops for natural scenes demands and requires complex analysis of image processing and segmentation algorithms, since these computational methods evaluate and predict environment physical characteristics, such as color elements, complex objects composition, shadows, brightness and inhomogeneous region colors for texture, JSEG segmentation algorithm was approached to segment these ones, and ANN and Bayes recognition models to classify images into predetermined classes (e.g. fruits, plants and general crops). The intended approach to segment classification deploys a customized MLP topology to classify and characterize the segments, which deals with a supervised learning by error correction – propagation of pattern inputs with changes in synaptic weights in a cyclic processing, with accurate recognition as well as easy parameter adjustment, as an enhancement of iRPROP algorithm (*improved resilient back-propagation*) (Igel and Hüsken, 2003) derived from *Back-propagation* algorithm, which has a faster identification mapping process, that verifies what region maps have similar matches through the explored environment. Bayes statistical models had the addiction of process variable as set parameters of predictive error correction.

To carry through this task, a feature vector is necessary for color channels histograms (layers of primary color in a digital image with a counting graph that measures how many pixels are at each level between black and white). After training process, the mean squared error

(MSE), denotes the best results achieved by segment classification to create the image-class map, which represents the segments into distinct feature vectors. Furthermore, a language dictionary is used for the expansion on main results, which semantic regions and negation detection are applied as data mining process with cognitive and statistical classifiers.

2. JSEG image segmentation

Color images with homogeneous regions are segmented with an algorithm to generate clusters in the color space/class (different measures classes in spectral distribution, with distinct intensity of visible electro-magnetic radiation at many discrete wavelengths) (Deng *et* al, 1999a). One way to segment images with textures is to consider the spatial arrangement of pixels using a region-growing technique whereby a homogeneity mode is defined with pixels grouped in the segmented region. Furthermore, in order to segment texture images one must consider different scales of images.

The JSEG algorithm segments images of natural scenes properly, without manual parameter adjustment for each image and simplifies texture and color. Segmentation with this algorithm passes through three stages, namely color space quantization (number reduction process of distinct colors in a given image), hit rate regions and similar color regions merging.

In the first stage, the color space is quantized with little perceptual degradation by using the quantization algorithm (Deng *et* al, 1999b) with minimum coloring. Each color is associated with a class. The original image pixels are replaced by classes to form the class maps in the next stage. Before performing the hit rate regions, the J-image - a class map for each windowed color region, whose positive and negative values represent the edges and textures of the processing image - must be created with pixel values used as a similarity algorithm for the hit rate region. These values are called „J-values" and are calculated from a window placed on the quantized image, where the J-value belongs.

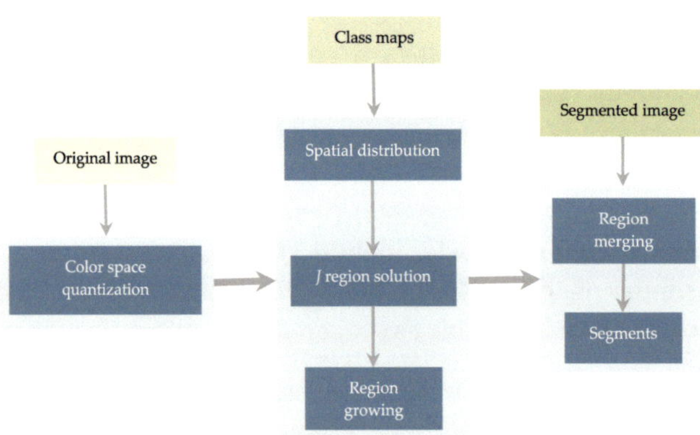

Figure 1. JSEG image segmentation steps.

http://dx.doi.org/10.5772/51862

2.1. Segmentation algorithm evaluation

Natural scenes present a 24-bit chromatic resolution color image, which is coarsely quantized preserving its major quality. The main idea for a good segmentation criterion is to extract representative colors differentiating neighboring regions in the acquired image, as an unsupervised method.

Therewith, the color quantization using peer group filtering (Deng *et al.*, 2001) is applied through perceptual weighting on individual pixels, to smooth the image and remove the existing noise. Then, new values indicating the smoothness of the local areas are obtained, and a weight is assigned to each pixel, prioritizing textured areas to smooth areas. These areas are identified with a quantization vector to the pixel colors, based on General Lloyd Algorithm (GLA) (Gersho and Gray, 1999), which the perceptually uniform L*u*v color space is adopted, presenting the overall distortion D:

$$D = \sum_{i} D_i = \sum_{i}\sum_{n} v(n)\left\|x(n) - c_i\right\|^2 \rightarrow x(n) \in C_i \tag{1}$$

And it is derived for:

$$c_i = \frac{\sum v(n)x(n)}{\sum v(n)} \rightarrow x(n) \in C_i \tag{2}$$

The parameters: c_i is the centroid of cluster C_i, $x(n)$ and $v(n)$ are the color vector and the perceptual weight for pixel n. D_i is the total distortion for C_i.

With the centroid value, as denoted by Equation (2) - after the vector quantization and merged clusters, pixels with the same color have two or more clusters, affected by GLA global distortion. For merging close clusters with minimum distance between preset thresholds for two centroids, an agglomerative clustering algorithm is performed on c_i (Duda and Hart, 1970), as the quantization parameter needed for spatial distribution.

After clustering merging for color quantization, a label is assigned for each quantized color, representing a color class for image pixels quantized to the same color. The image pixel colors are replaced by their corresponding color class labels, creating a class-map.

In order to calculate the J-value, Z is defined as the set of all points of quantized image, then $z = (x, y)$ with $z \in Z$ and being m the average in all Z elements. C is the number of classes obtained in the quantization. Then Z is classified into C classes, Z_i are the elements of Z belonging to class i, where $i=1,\ldots,C$, and m_i are the element averages in Z_i.

$$m_i = \frac{1}{N_i}\sum_{z \in Z} z \tag{3}$$

The J-value is as follows:

$$J = \frac{S_B}{S_W} = \frac{(S_T - S_W)}{S_W} \tag{4}$$

where:

$$S_T = \sum_{z \in Z} \left\| z - m \right\|^2 \tag{5}$$

$$S_W = \sum_{i=1}^{C} \sum_{z \in Z} \left\| z - m_i \right\|^2 \tag{6}$$

The parameter S_T represents the sum of quantized image points within the average in all Z elements. Thereby, the relation between S_B and S_W, denotes the measures of distances of this class relation, for arbitrary nonlinear class distributions. J for higher values indicates an increasing distance between the classes and points for each other, considering images with homogeneous color regions. The distance and consequently, the J value, decrease for images with uniformly color classes.

Each segmented region could be recalculated, instead of the entire class-map, with new parameters adjustment for $\bar{J}$ average. J_K represents J calculated over region k, M_k is the number of points in region k, N is the total number of points in the class-map, with all regions in class-map summation.

$$\bar{J} = \frac{1}{N} \sum_{k} M_k J_k \tag{7}$$

For a fixed number of regions, a criterion for $\bar{J}$ is intended for lower values.

2.2. Spatial segmentation technique

The global minimization of $\bar{J}$ is not practical, if not applied to a local area of the class-map. Therefore, the idea of *J-image* is the generation of a gray-scale image whose pixel values are the J values calculated over local windows centered on these pixels. With a higher value for J-image, the pixel should be near region boundaries.

Expected local windows dimensions determines the size of image regions, for intensity and color edges in smaller sizes, and the opposite occurs detecting texture boundaries.

Using a region-growing method to segment the image, this one is considered initially as one single region. The algorithm for spatial segmentation starts segment all the regions in the image at an initial large scale until the minimum specified scale is reached. This final scale is settled manually for the appropriate image size. The initial scale 1 corresponds to 64x64 image size, scale 2 to 128x128 image size, scale 3 to 256x256 image size, with due proportion for increasing scales and the double image size.

http://dx.doi.org/10.5772/51862

Below, the spatial segmentation algorithm is structured in flow steps.

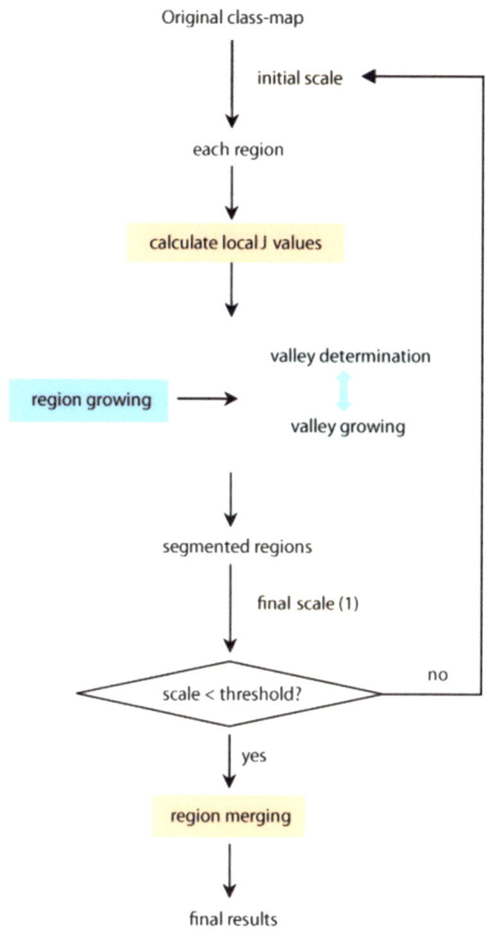

Figure 2. Sequence for spatial segmentation algorithm.

3. Image processing (spatial distribution and objects quantification)

The sequential images evince not only the color quantization (spatial distributions forming a map of classes), but also the space segmentation (J-image representing edges and regions of textured side).

Several window sizes are used by J-values: the largest detects the region boundaries by referring to texture parameters; the lowest detects changes in color and/or intensity of light. Each window size is associated with a scale image analysis. The concept of J-image, together with different scales, allows the segmentation of regions by referring to texture parameters.

Regions with the lowest values of J-image are called valleys. The lowest values are applied with a heuristic algorithm. Thus, it is possible to determine the starting point of efficient growth, which depends on the addition of similar valleys. The algorithm ends when there are spare pixels to be added to those regions.

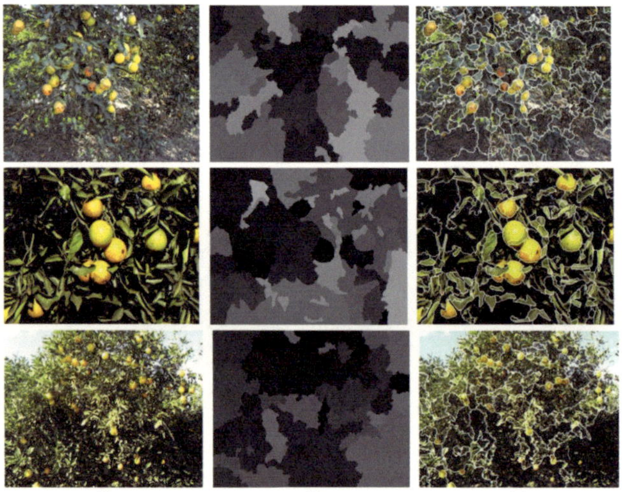

(a) (b) (c)

Figure 3. a) Original images; (b) Color quantization (map of classes); (c) J-image representing edges and regions of textured side (Spatial distributions).

It was observed that the oranges represent the largest number of image pixels, given its characteristics of high contrast with other objects on the scene.

Fig. 3, above, shows three types of scenes in orchards. The first identifies the largest part of the tree. In this category, the quantization threshold was adjusted to higher values for the fusion of regions with same color tone between branches, leaves and ground would be avoided. The second scene denotes the regions' set details in orchards, excluding darker regions. Not only irregularities of each leaf are segmented, as well as abnormalities of color tones in fruit itself, allowing later analysis of disease characteristics. The third category identifies most of the trees, but with higher incidence of top and bottom regions.

4. Artificial Neural Networks (ANN) – MLP customized algorithm

It is fundamental that an ANN-based classification method associated with a statistical pattern recognition be used. *Multi-Layer Perceptron* (MLP) (Haykin, 1999; Haykin, 2008) is suitable for default ANN topology to be implemented through a customized *back-propagation* algorithm for complex patterns (Costa and Cesar Junior, 2001).

The most appropriate segment and topology classifications are those using vectors extracted from HSV color space (Hue, Saturation, Value), matching RGB color space (Red, Green,

Blue) components. Also, the network with less MSE in the neurons to color space proportion is used to classify the entities.

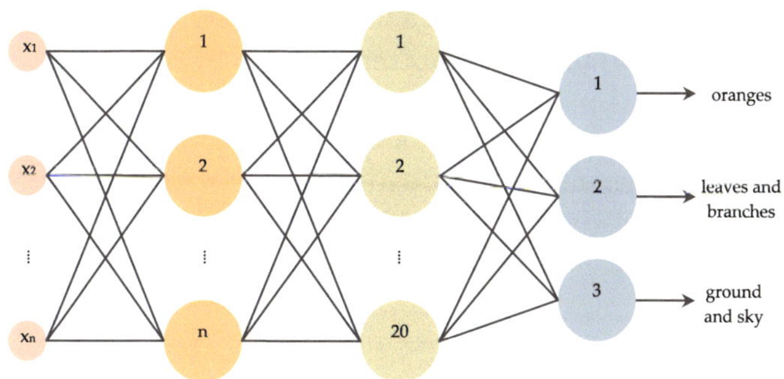

Figure 4. ANN schematic topology for fruits with three classes.

Derived from back-propagation, the iRPROP algorithm (improved resilient back-propagation) (Lulio, 2010) is both fast and accurate, with easy parameter adjustment. It features an Octave (Eaton, 2006) module which was adopted for the purposes of this work and it is classified with HSV (H – hue, S – saturation, V – value) color space channels histograms of 256 categories (32, 64,128 and 256 neurons in a hidden layer training for each color space channel: H, HS, and HSV). The output layer has three neurons, each of them having a predetermined class.

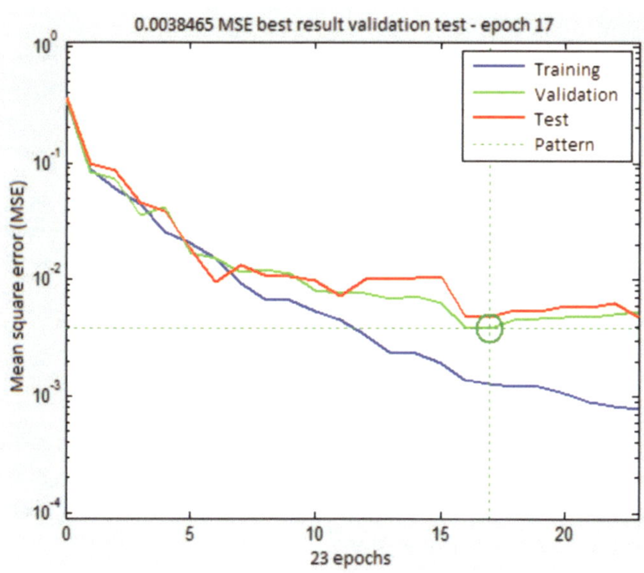

Figure 5. MSE 50% validation tests for RGB.

The charts below (Figures 5, 6, 7, 8) denote the ratio of mean square error (MSE) and amount of times to obtain the best performance index during the validation data towards the training and test sets.

All ANN-based topologies are trained with a threshold lower than 0.0001 mean squared errors (MSE), the synaptic neurons weights are initiated with random values and the other algorithm parameters were set with Fast Artificial Neural Network (FANN) library (Nissen, 2006) for Matlab (Mathworks Inc.) platform, and also its Neural Network toolbox. The most appropriate segment and topology classifications are those using vectors extracted from HSV color space. Also, a network with less MSE in the H-64 was used so as to classify the planting area; for class navigable area (soil), HSV-256 was chosen; as for the class sky, the HS-32.

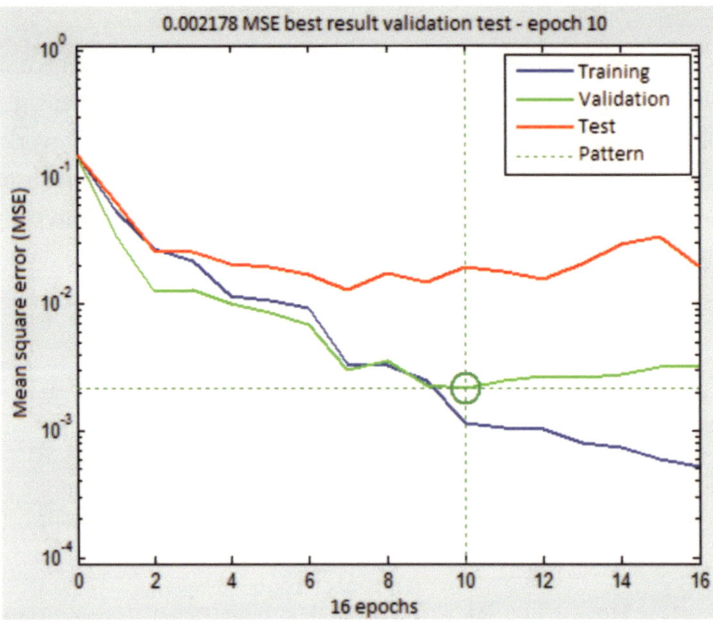

Figure 6. MSE 100% validation tests for RGB.

Figures 9 and 10 denote the regression for target-outputs of ANN classifier, for RGB and HSV classes. The higher the concentration of data at the intersection of bias and Y = T (equal to the output sampling period), the lower the linear regression of data is classified, based on confusion matrices for each set of dimensions.

The response times are given for combinations of training, testing, validation and all data sets.

http://dx.doi.org/10.5772/51862

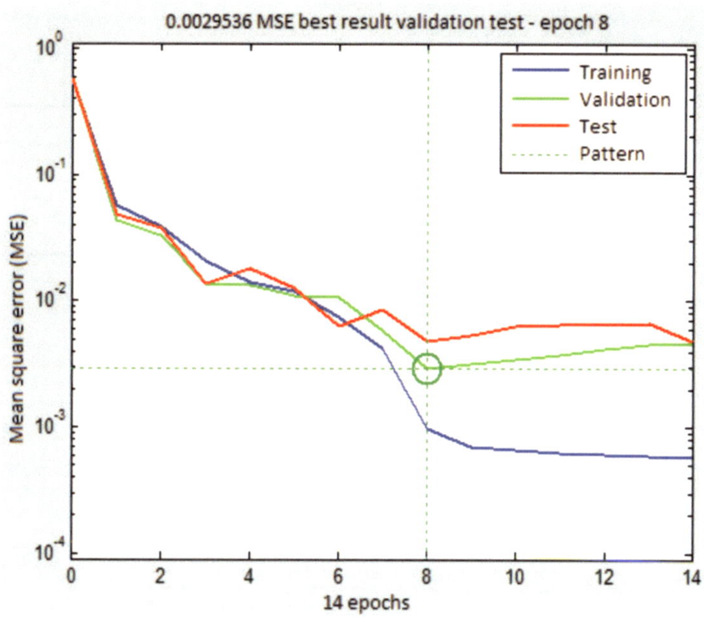

Figure 7. MSE 50% validation tests for HSV.

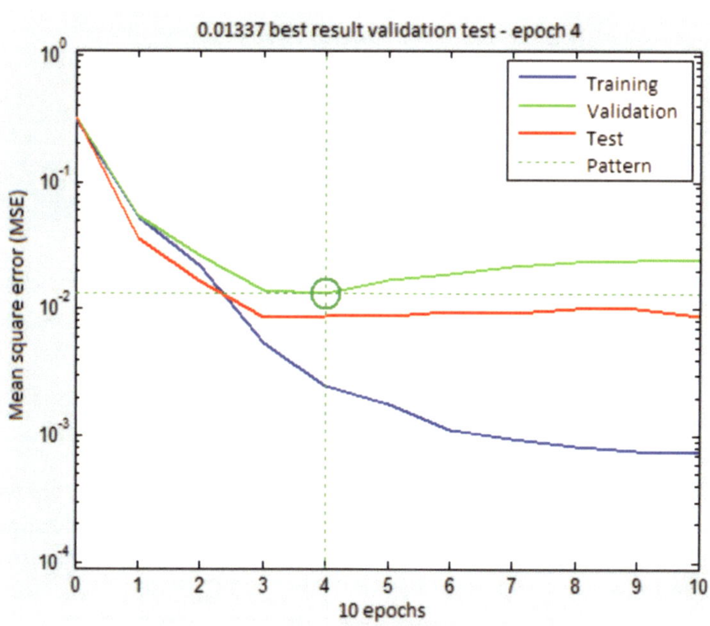

Figure 8. MSE 100% validation tests for HSV.

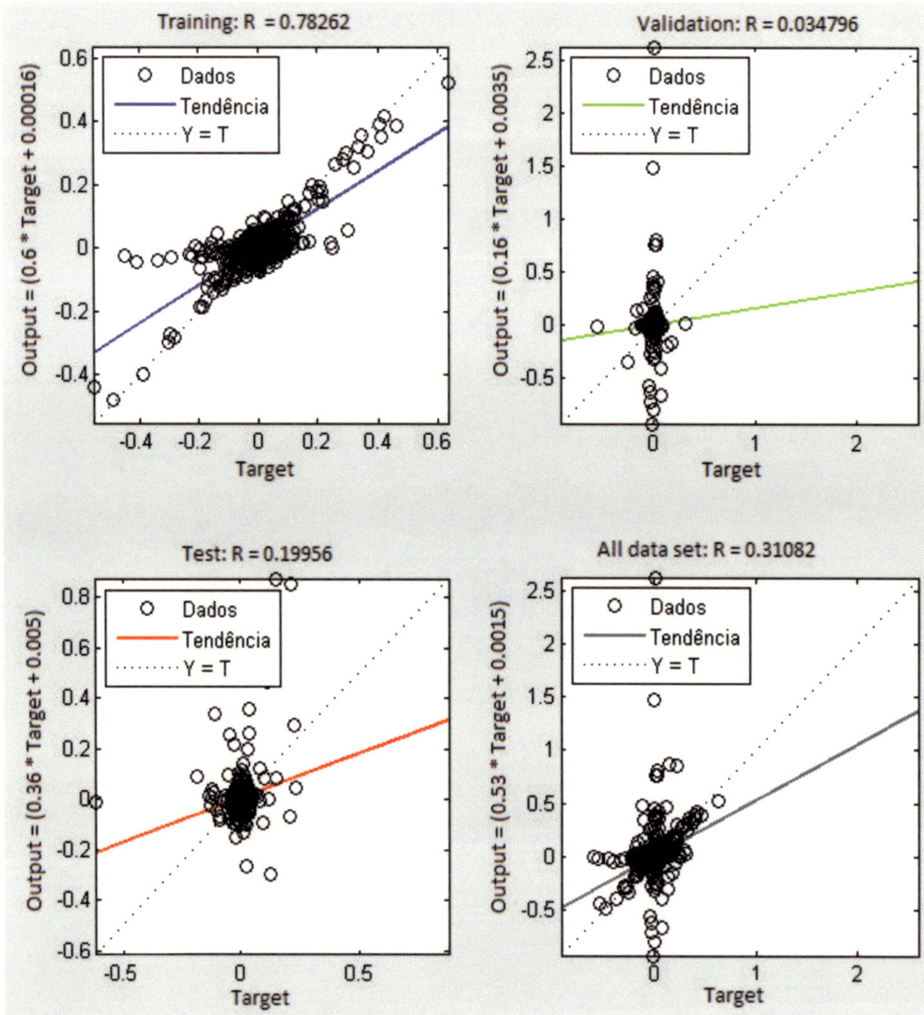

Figure 9. MSE 50% (left) and 100% (right) validation tests for RGB.

5. Statistical pattern recognition

Statistical methods are employed as a combination of results with ANN, showing how accuracy in non-linear features vectors can be best applied in a MLP algorithm with a statistical improvement, which processing speed is essentially important, for pattern classification. *Bayes Theorem* and *Naive Bayes* (Comaniciu and Meer, 1997) both use a technique for iterations inspection, namely MCA (*Main Component Analysis*), which uses a linear transformation that minimizes co-variance while it maximizes variance. Features found through this transformation are totally uncorrelated, so the redundancy between them is avoided. Thus, the components (features) represent the key information contained in data, reducing the number of dimensions. Therefore, RGB space color is used to compare the total number of dimensions in feature vectors with HSV. With a smaller dimension of iterations, HSV is chosen as the default space color in most applications (Grasso and Recce, 1996).

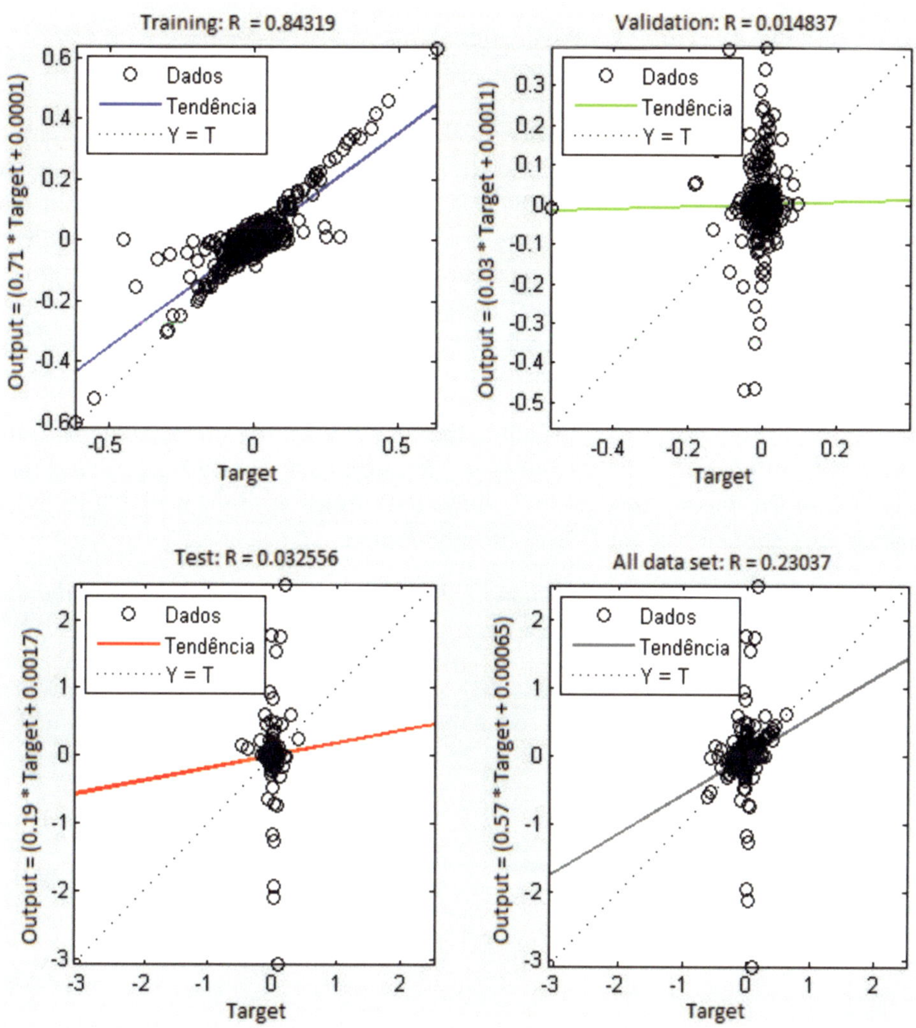

Figure 10. MSE 50% (left) and 100% (right) validation tests for RGB.

Bayes Theorem introduces a modified mathematical equation for the Probability Density Function (PDF), which estimates the training set in a conditional statistics. Equation (8) denotes the solution for $p(C_i|y)$ relating the PDF to conditional class i (classes in natural scene), and y is a n-dimensional feature vector. *Naive Bayes* implies independence for vector features, what means that each class assumes the conditional parameter for the PDF, following Equation (9) (Morimoto *et* al, 2000).

$$P(C_i \mid y) = \frac{p(y \mid C_i)P(C_i)}{\sum_{j=1}^{K} p(y \mid C_j)P(C_j)} \tag{8}$$

$$P(y \mid C_i) = \prod_{j=1}^{n} p(y_j \mid C_i) \tag{9}$$

In Fig. 11, for the location of fruits in the RGB case, the discrimination of the classes fruit, sky and leaves, twigs and branches, attends constant amounts proportional to the increasing of the training sets. This amount, for HSV case, is reduced for the fruit class, as the dispersion of pixels is greater in this color space. In Fig. 12, in the RGB case, the best results were obtained using Bayes classifier, having smaller ratio estimation in relation to the number of components analyzed. In this color space, the estimation in the recognition of objects related to the fruits is given by the PDF of each dimension, correcting the current values by the hope of each area not matched to the respective class.

Also in Fig. 12, the recognition of the fruit to the HSV case presents balance in the results of the two classifiers, but with a compensation of the success rate, for lower margins of the estimation ratio to the Bayes classifier. This allows the correction of the next results by priori estimation approximating, in the PDF of each dimension.

It can be seen that, the ratio of the estimation must be lesser for the increasing of the dimensions number and its subsequent classification, in all cases.

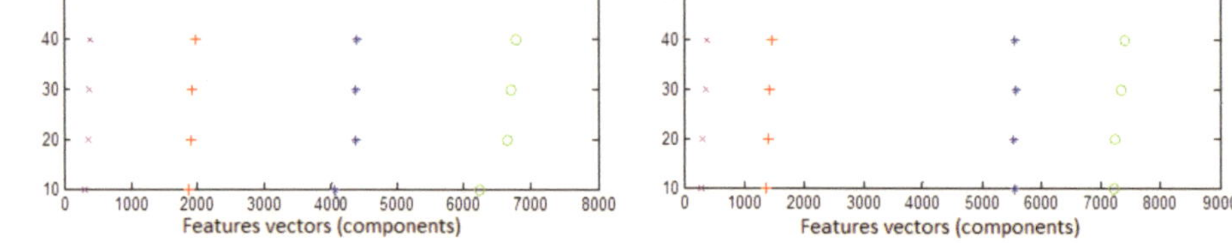

Figure 11. Quantity of dimensions of each set (oranges RGB - left, oranges HSV - right).

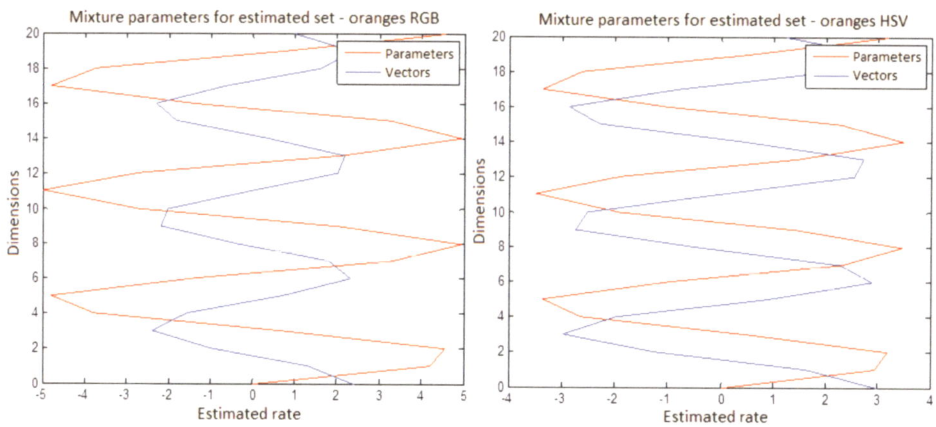

Figure 12. Mixture parameters for estimated set (oranges RGB - left, oranges HSV - right).

6. Objects quantification (post-processing)

The classes maps are processed, as the representation by the area filling (*floodfill*) brings only solid regions which are quantified. Initially, a conversion is performed on gray level image in order to threshold regions that are outlined. Then, to determine the labels of the elements connected, it is necessary to exclude objects which are greater than 200 to 300 pixels, depending on the focal length. Thus, it is necessary to identify each element smaller than this threshold, and calculate the properties of these objects, such as area, centroid, and the boundary region. As a result, the objects that present areas near the circular geometry will be labelled and quantified as fruits.

To determine the metrics and the definition of objects of orange crop, the graph-based segmentation (Gonzalez and Woods, 2007) was applied. This technique provides the adjacency relation between the binary values of the pixels, and their respective positions, highlighting the local geometric properties of the image.

In first case, areas corresponding to small regions, as fruits partially hidden (oranges) with equivalent texture and color properties to leaves are excluded. Then, estimated elements are fully grouped, when overlap the representative segments, which denote an orange fruit. Lastly, the grouping is applied for regions which detect two or more representative segments, denoting another orange fruit.

As the best classification results, related to second approach were through Bayes in HSV color space, only the maps of class from these classifiers will be presented to localization and quantification of objects, compared to RGB case.

Then, for the RGB and HSV cases are presented, through Figures 13 to 21, the images in their respective maps of class, the pre-processing for thresholding with areas smaller than

100 and greater than 300, the geometric approximation metrics for the detection of circular objects, the boundary regions with the centroid of each object, and finally the label associated to the fruit.

Figure 13. Maps of RGB (left) and HSV (right) classes - scene 1.

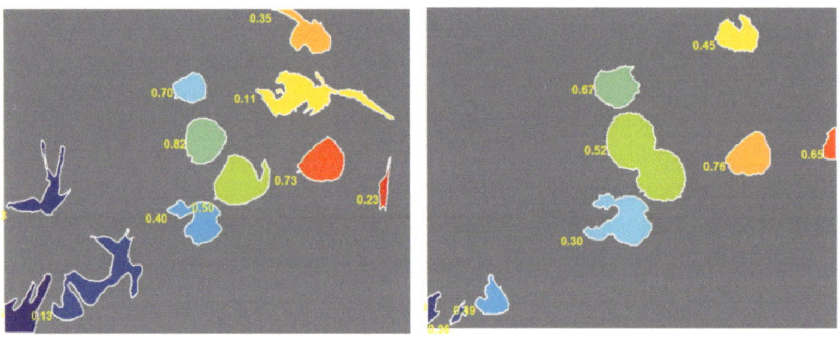

Figure 14. Metric near circular geometry threshold 1.0 for RGB (left) and HSV (right) - scene 1.

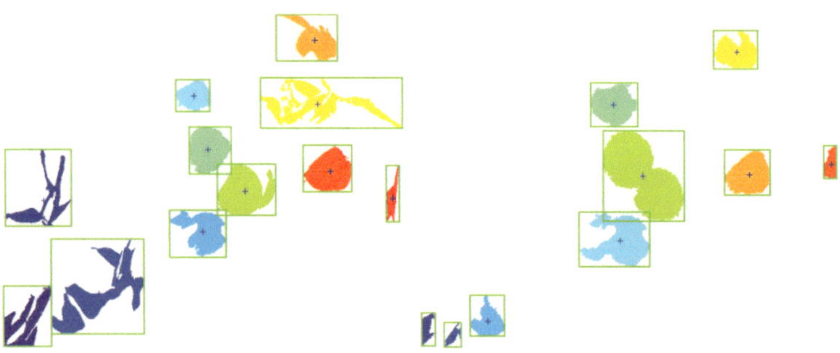

Figure 15. Representation of area and centroid for fruit association in two cases - scene 1.

http://dx.doi.org/10.5772/51862

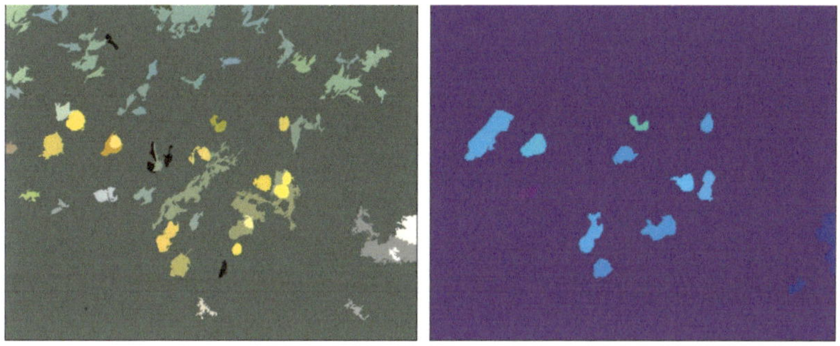

Figure 16. Maps of RGB (left) and HSV (right) classes - scene 2.

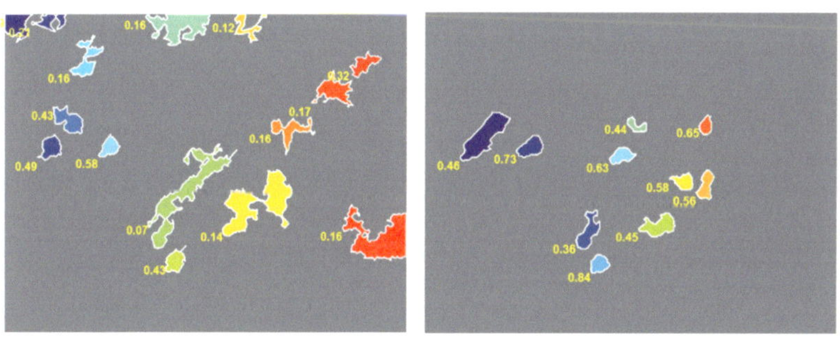

Figure 17. Metric near circular geometry threshold 1.0 for RGB (left) and HSV (right) - scene 2.

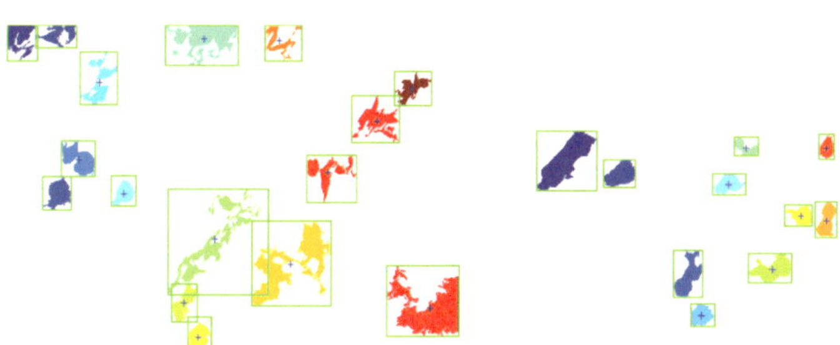

Figure 18. Representation of area and centroid for fruit association in two cases - scene 2.

Figure 19. Maps of RGB (left) and HSV (right) classes - scene 3.

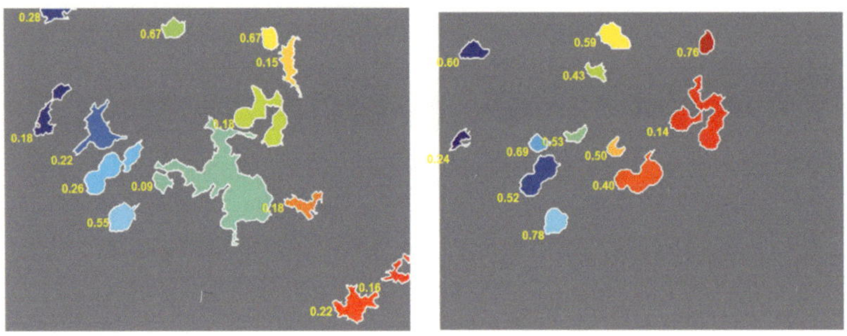

Figure 20. Metric near circular geometry threshold 1.0 for RGB (left) and HSV (right) - scene 3.

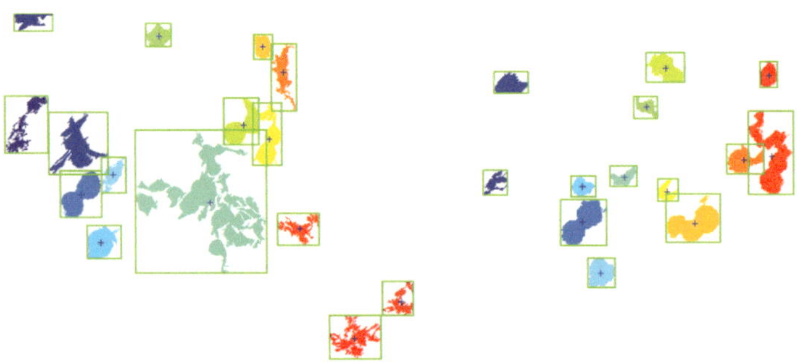

Figure 21. Representation of area and centroid for fruit association in two cases - scene 3.

7. Conclusions

This chapter presented merging techniques for segmentation and statistical classification of agricultural orange crops scenes, running multiple segmentation tests with JSEG algorithm possible. As the data provided evince, this generated algorithms fulfills the expectations as far as segmenting is concerned, so that it sorts the appropriate classes (fruits; leaves and branches; sky). As a result, a modular strategy with Bayes statistical theorem can be an option for the classification of segments applied with cognitive approach.

Author details

Luciano Cássio Lulio[1], Mário Luiz Tronco[1], Arthur José Vieira Porto[1],
Carlos Roberto Valêncio[2] and Rogéria Cristiane Gratão de Souza[2]

1 Engineering School of Sao Carlos, University of Sao Paulo (EESC/USP), Sao Carlos, São Paulo, Brazil

2 Statistical and Computing Science Department, State University of Sao Paulo (DCCE/UNESP), São Jose do Rio Preto, São Paulo, Brazil

References

[1] Comaniciu, D., & Meer, P. (1997). Robust analysis of feature spaces: color image segmentation. In: Conference on Computer Vision and Pattern Recognition, IEEE Computer Society

[2] Costa, L. F., & Cesar, Junior. R. M. (2001). Shape analysis and classification- Theory and Practice. 1. ed. Boca Raton, Florida, EUA: CRC Press LLC. 0-84933-493-4

[3] Deng, Y., Kennedy, C., Moore, M. S., & Manjunath, B. S. (1999a). Peer group filtering and perceptual color image quantization. Proceedings of the 1999 IEEE International Symposium on Circuits and Systems, , 4, 21-25.

[4] Deng, Y., Manjunath, B. S., & Shin, H. (1999b). Color image segmentation. Conference on Computer Vision and Pattern Recognition, IEEE Computer Society, , 2, 446-451.

[5] Deng, Y., & Manjunath, B. S. (2001). Unsupervised segmentation of color-texture regions in images and videos. IEEE Transactions on Pattern Analysis and Machine Intelligence (PAMI'01), , 23(8), 800-810.

[6] Duda, R. O., & Hart, P. E. (1970). Pattern Classification and Scene Analysis, John Wiley & Sons, New York

[7] Eaton, J. W., et al. (2006). Octave. Avaliable at: http://www.octave.org

[8] Gersho, A., & Gray, R. M. (1992). Vector quantization and signal compression, Kluwer Academic, Norwell, MA

[9] Gonzalez, R. C., & Woods, R. E. (2007). Digital Image Processing. 3 ed. New Jersey, EUA: Prentice-Hall Inc

[10] Grasso, G. M., & Recce, M. (1996). Scene Analysis for an Orange Picking Robot,"In: International Congress for Computer Technology in Agri-culture

[11] Haykin, S. (1999). Neural networks: a comprehensive foundation. 2. ed. New Jersey, EUA: Prentice-Hall. 0-13273-350-1

[12] Haykin, S. (2008). Neural Networks and Learning Machines. 3.ed. McMaster University, Canada: Prentice-Hall. 0-13147-139-2

[13] Igel, C., & Hüsken, M. (2003). Empirical evaluation of the improved Rprop learning algorithm. Neurocomputing, , 50, 105-123.

[14] Lulio, L. C. (2011). Computer vision techniques applied to natural scenes recognition and autonomous locomotion of agricultural mobile robots. São Carlos, 353 p. Dissertation (Master of Science)- School of Engineering of São Carlos, University of São Paulo, São Carlos

[15] Morimoto, T., Takeuchi, T., Miyata, H., & Hashimoto, Y. (2000). Pattern recognition of fruit shapes based on the concept of chaos and neural networks,"Computers and Electronics in Agriculture, , 26, 171-186.

[16] Nissen, S., et al. (2006). Fann: fast artificial neural network library. Avaliable at: http://leenissen.dk/fann/